Are You Sad Too?

Helping Children Deal with Loss and Death

Dinah Seibert, MS
Judy C. Drolet, PhD, CHES
Joyce V. Fetro, PhD, CHES

Suggestions for teachers, parents and other care providers of children to age 10

ETR ASSOCIATES
Santa Cruz, California
1993

ETR Associates (Education, Training and Research) is a nonprofit organization committed to fostering the health, well-being and cultural diversity of individuals, families, schools and communities. The publishing program of ETR Associates provides books and materials that empower young people and adults with the skills to make positive health choices. We invite health professionals to learn more about our high-quality publishing, training and research programs by contacting us at P.O. Box 1830, Santa Cruz, CA 95061-1830.

10 9 8 7 6 5 4

Printed in the United States of America

Illustrations by Marcia Quackenbush
Design by Julia Chiapella and Ann Smiley

Library of Congress Cataloging-in-Publication Data

Seibert, Dinah.
    Are you sad too? : helping children deal with loss and death /
  Dinah Seibert, Judy C. Drolet, Joyce V. Fetro.
        p.   cm.
    Includes bibliographical references.
    ISBN 1-56071-117-5
    1. Children and death. 2. Death—Study and teaching (Elemen-
  tary). 3. Bereavement in children. 4. Children—Counseling of.
  I. Drolet, Judy Catherine, 1951– . II. Fetro, Joyce V. III. Title.
  BF723.D3S56   1993
  155.9'37'083—dc20   92-21150

Title No. 568

To all adults who have the courage to confront their own attitudes and beliefs toward death and to share them with the children in their lives.

To all the children encouraged by these adults to develop a healthy attitude toward death and a positive attitude toward everything life has to teach.

—DS, JCD, JVF

Contents

Preface

People who face the challenge of dealing directly with death often find strengths within themselves that they never knew existed. They may discover that they are truly up to the challenge. They may realize that personal growth can change their perspectives and add meaning to their lives.

Having witnessed this personal growth in ourselves, friends, loved ones and students, we developed a commitment to the need for death education. Our combined history convinced us that this topic is so important it must be shared.

Because we know that children can learn to understand death, because we have respect for their capacity to be resilient and face difficult experiences, and because we know that children can experience the same benefits in personal growth, we believe that death education should be shared with children as well as adults!

Since our professional approaches have always emphasized practical applications of concepts through teaching and writing, this book was a natural and exciting step for us. As we thought about the purpose of this book, we decided on these goals:

- To help parents, teachers, and caregivers become more comfortable with loss and death

- To give them permission to talk directly to children about loss and death

- To encourage them to help children learn the important lessons that loss teaches

- To provide them with a practical guide with manageable steps that can be adapted to a variety of situations and stages of growth

We hope that when you finish this book you will know what we know—that the process of sharing our loss and death experiences helps us cope with the immediate situation and learn lessons for a healthier future. Sharing our feelings, beliefs and knowledge with children nourishes all of our spirits—adults and children alike. As we share with children they learn to share with us, and we *all* improve our life skills, our compassion and our inner strengths.

Sharing loss and death experiences supports your spirit during difficult times the way a snowshoe supports your weight over deep snow. If all of your body weight is placed on one foot as you step into deep snow, you either fall through and get stuck or your steps are dragged down by the heaviness of the snow. But when your weight is spread over the area of a snowshoe, you are able to keep walking across the top of the snow almost unhindered.

If we try to bear a loss or death alone, we may find the weight too great to carry. We may be unable to cope with the daily traumas involved. But when we share the weight of our difficult tasks and emotions with others, it is easier to bear the hardships and find ways to cope with our losses.

We hope that our book can help you to find snowshoes that will carry you and your children through the losses in your lives to a fuller understanding of life.

Acknowledgments

Because this book has been stirring in us for such a long time, listing all those who had an influence on us is difficult. Probably many people in our past moved us toward this goal when we weren't even aware of it. Thus some of our acknowledgments are general, but all are quite sincere.

First, a thank you to the ETR Associates staff for their vision in recognizing the need for this book. We appreciate their involving and supporting us in its creation and development.

Special thanks to our editor, Kay Clark, for her expert technical assistance. Because of the sensitive nature of the content, Kay also provided valuable support and patience as we worked through more than just the printed words.

We offer our appreciation to all the children and adults, the Southern Illinois University at Carbondale (SIUC) health education students, and the friends who shared their experiences and broadened ours. Our thanks go especially to Dr. Robert Russell in the Department of Health Education at SIUC who was an early mentor in death education for us all. Through his courses and his friendship and teamwork, he provided us a foundation in the concepts of death education. He led us to the understanding that death education is really life education.

Our final thanks go to our families, who supported us professionally and personally so that we could take the steps to write this book. They provided the atmosphere we needed for our past explorations, and encouraged us in the effort to share our experience and knowledge with others.

Educating Children About Loss and Death

Loss and death are natural parts of life for children as well as adults. Children are not immune to loss. Their experiences range from a friend moving away or a cartoon character getting flattened to their parents divorcing or the death of a loved one. Their reactions to loss and death are as broad as their experiences. How do we know? Because they have questions!

When given the opportunity and an open atmosphere, children ask a great variety of questions about death. They develop important life skills through reacting and questioning. They practice using the language and feeling the feelings on their way to mastering coping skills. It's up to us as parents and teachers to provide opportunities and an open atmosphere where children can practice these skills and learn to see death as a natural part of life.

You're not alone if you don't feel prepared for this responsibility! Neither parents nor teachers are likely to have had preparation for dealing with the subject of death. Death is one of the taboo topics in our society; thus, it is normal to feel uncomfortable talking about death.

Preparing to talk about death means gaining knowledge and getting comfortable with your feelings. An understanding of biological death is important. But possibly more important is an understanding of the language, traditions, rituals, religious beliefs and feelings associated with death. It's good to take time to explore your own experiences, spirituality and feelings when you are not in the midst of a death-related crisis, when you will be able to reflect more objectively.

A personal awareness of loss and death will help you be more comfortable in encouraging children to explore these subjects. There is no good time to lose a loved one, and you can't really prepare for the grief you will experience. But you can learn coping skills that make the grief more bearable. Once you have acknowledged your own feelings and beliefs, you will be able to make death a more comfortable topic when the children in your life have questions.

As you become more comfortable talking about death, however, you may notice that people around you become *uncomfortable!* They may even label you as "morbid" or "strange." Or they may just avoid discussing the topic with you. Because of this pressure to keep death quiet, it takes a special strength and determination to prepare yourself to encourage and support children as they explore death.

This book is written to help you and the children you care about learn more about life by talking about loss and death. We'll show how death education for children can become life education for everyone involved. Learning to cope with loss and death is a life skill that must be taught and nurtured.

The Case for Death Education

Learning and sharing about death aren't easy tasks. So it's important for you to be clear about why death education is a good idea for children. Part of the taboo of death is seen in the way well-meaning adults attempt to shield children from death. In his article "Explaining Death to Children: The Healing Process," Garanzini (1987) makes this dramatic case in favor of sharing death experiences with children:

> Attempts to shield children from the reality of death reinforces in them the perception that death is either not real, too frightening to examine or, worst of all that the ending of life is not worth noting with respect and reverence. These unintended lessons are unhealthy....For the sake of a healthy,...sound appreciation of the meaning of death, parents and teachers must face the topic realistically and naturally—for themselves and for the children they teach (p.30).

Confusion and isolation caused by shielding children from important life events like loss and death creates an unhealthy stress that can interrupt their growth and development. When these issues are acknowledged and dealt with directly, however, children are able to observe role models, practice coping skills, and learn fully from their life experiences.

Without an adult to listen, explain and comfort a child, the lessons are not simply lost—they are harmful. Children are "excellent observers, and poor interpreters" (Garanzini, 1987). A child's imagination is often much worse than the reality. If you don't talk about death, children will find this absence mysterious and make up a reason for your silence. Or suppose the child gets incorrect information from an influential television show. How will the child be able to see the reality or straighten out the facts without an encouraging, direct and honest adult interpreter? Your role as parent or teacher or interpreter is to use the child's daily life experiences to help teach life skills, including coping with death.

With your help, in small steps, children can learn to express and share their grief. Little by little they can come to understand that death is a natural part of life, thus mastering an important life skill.

The case for death education for children is clear. In educating children about loss and death, parents and teachers:

- acknowledge and share children's feelings

- prevent the often unintended but potentially harmful side-effects of ignoring children's interest in death

- promote positive emotional development by giving children the ability to cope with even the most difficult aspects of life

Knowing What to Teach

The goal of this book is to help you present a positive view of death in your interactions with children. To help you do this we have drawn on a broad background of research and personal and professional experience to help you prepare for talking to children about death. In this book you'll find the foundation you'll need, including:

- terms most often used

- an understanding of the stages children go through as they develop their ideas about death

- ways that children experience death
- influences on children's perceptions

When you talk to children about death, it is important that you present a positive view of death. But what does that mean? A positive presentation of death is a view that

- is factually accurate
- is appropriate for the child's level of understanding
- creates a healthy understanding of death as a natural part of life rather than promoting fear and misunderstanding

Before you can determine what is appropriate for the child's level of understanding you must learn how that understanding changes with experience and age. Children's concepts of death become increasingly more detailed, realistic and factual over time. They move from the view that death is temporary, reversible, and happens only to others, to the understanding that death is final, irreversible, and happens to everyone. These different levels of understanding translate into very different interests and questions about death.

Once you know how to assess children's abilities, you can move on to deciding what is appropriate to talk about.

Four Areas of Death Education

If you are a teacher planning a thorough death education curriculum you will want to include lessons in four important areas—*facts, feelings, beliefs* and *coping skills*. It is important for adults to share their feelings and beliefs with children. And the feelings and beliefs of children must be shared, explored and accepted. Matters such as causes of death, and funeral and burial rituals ought to be explained honestly and directly. And, finally, children need role models and support as they learn skills for coping with death.

As parents or teachers responding to a current death, you may choose to focus on only one of these four areas. For death education to be most beneficial, however, children will eventually need to deal with all four areas in the course of their exploration. Chapter 3 will give you more details about what children need to know about death.

How to Use This Book

All the significant adults in a child's life may become involved with death education experiences. Whether you're the teacher, parent, caregiver, minister, neighbor, relative or friend, this book is designed for you.

So far, we've been talking about ideal situations where planning allows lessons to be given at a pace everyone can manage. A much more common situation occurs when a child either acts out or asks questions in response to an actual death. This is a classic example of "the teachable moment," when parents and teachers must be prepared to focus on whatever aspects are on the minds of the children. Providing immediate emotional support is usually the most important task. But if the children are asking factual questions instead of struggling with emotions, then direct, factual answers are needed. Sometimes professional help is needed. Learning to distinguish between situations you can handle and situations where you need help is most important.

Children are experiencing loss and death regularly. Their experiences may range from changing schools to the death of a bug or a flower to a parent becoming disabled or even the death of a loved one. When children experience loss, they're getting practice at bearing unpleasant feelings like the ones that occur when they experience a death.

Although the time frame and the intensity will vary, the process of grieving and adjusting to a new life situation is the same for any loss or death. Even small losses like wilting flowers or torn teddy bears can teach children big lessons when there is a respectful adult who will listen, explain and comfort. Whatever their experiences, children are learning from them. Unfortunate yet necessary lessons will occur— children will learn to bear unpleasantness and survive difficult situations.

Parts of the book, such as Chapter 5, Using Planned Learning Activities, are directed primarily toward teachers, while Chapter 6, Responding to a Loss or a Death, is directed more toward parents. Try not to be limited by the phrasing of the ideas. Think about the concepts and about ways to adapt the materials for use in your specific situation. As you read, you'll find suggestions for adults in a variety of roles.

We believe you'll get the most out of this book if you read it completely before putting the ideas into action. When you have the foundation and the "big picture," use individual sections and suggestions as you need them.

Chapter 1 walks you through a personal assessment of your own experiences, feelings and beliefs related to death. Use this self-assessment to prepare yourself emotionally and personally for your work with children. It also will help you become comfortable with the language and concepts used in death education.

In Chapter 2 you will learn how children develop their understanding of death in different stages and what the characteristics of each stage are. This chapter also examines the various influences that inform and shape children's views of death.

Chapter 3 looks at what children need to know about death. It is divided into the four areas to be explored: facts, feelings, beliefs and coping skills. After this background, you'll find ways to explore each of the four areas and how to decide which area is most appropriate for your specific situation. This chapter will also help you be thorough if you are developing a death-education program.

Chapter 4 provides guidelines for discussing death with children and examples of questions children may ask. The sample answers provided model the concepts discussed throughout this book.

In Chapter 5 you will find suggestions for implementing planned learning activities about death, and specific activities to use. The activities section is organized around the four areas described in Chapter 3.

Chapter 6 offers support and suggestions for what to do if a loss or death occurs in the lives of your children. It discusses the stages of grief and the points to consider in your response, then offers detailed, specific responses for a variety of situations, ranging from the loss of a toy to the death of a parent.

If you want to use children's literature to help you teach about death, Chapter 7 provides suggestions. Several books are recommended, followed by a summary of each story and a discussion of the important death education concepts illustrated by the story. In order to provide this annotation, we have included only books with which we are familiar, not a complete list.

If you've exhausted the contents of this book, or you're interested in more detail on a specific concept, see the Suggested Readings section at the end of the book to find out where to start your additional reading. All research referred to in this book is documented in the References. The glossary at the end of the book provides definitions of various terms used in the book.

As You Begin...

As you begin your exploration of death as a natural part of life, be alert to the positive messages below. These messages are woven throughout this book like threads: threads that tie positive views of death to positive and healthy emotional development in children.

It is important for adults to help young children explore death concepts because

- death is a natural part of a child's life
- coping with death is a critical life skill
- children have questions about death
- ignoring or denying death is unhealthy and
- acknowledging death is healthy

Before you begin sharing your knowledge, feelings and beliefs about death with children, be sure to

- understand that children learn about death in small steps over time
- recognize the influences on your own perceptions of death
- identify the numerous influences on children's perceptions of death

Finally, when helping children explore death concepts, it is important to

- use the child's daily experiences
- create an open atmosphere where the topic of death is not uncomfortable
- use direct, factual language
- acknowledge and accept children's feelings and beliefs
- avoid trauma or judgment
- include children in death-related rituals or ceremonies as their interest and understanding allows

Chapter 1

Reviewing Your History of Death Experiences

The first step in helping children cope with loss and death is to create an open atmosphere where children's feelings and questions are accepted—where death is not a hidden topic. When you feel afraid or not competent to respond to children's feelings, children quickly learn not to express these feelings openly. If you answer their questions with whispers or with anger, children learn not to ask them. Although not always able to explain their reactions, children are quick to understand when they are making adults uncomfortable. And when adults are uncomfortable, children typically don't feel free to explore concepts in their normally expressive and questioning manner.

Since loss and death are extremely personal life situations, you are sharing your own beliefs, experiences and feelings when you discuss death. You may not *plan* to and you may not be *aware* that you are doing this; but you need to know that you *are*. The way life and death have affected you will influence the way you respond to the beliefs, experiences and feelings of the children in your life.

Before you can help children explore their concepts of death, you must explore your own beliefs and biases stemming from your family background and culture, your long-term history with loss and death, and your specific experiences. As you explore each concept, you'll begin to understand its impact on your feelings and actions related to death.

Looking at your *beliefs* about life after death and funeral rituals will help you see how your religious or nonreligious background contributes to an attitude about what happens, or should happen, when someone dies. *Having* a specific bias or cultural perspective is not a strength or a weakness; it is simply a fact. Being *aware* of your own perspectives and of the diversity of perspectives in your community is a strength.

Teacher and parent roles in the area of belief will differ, of course. Because beliefs related to death come from very personal religious and cultural backgrounds, the role of a parent is to teach and reinforce personal beliefs. But because classrooms may include children from a broad variety of religious and cultural backgrounds, the role of a teacher is to teach and accept the variety of beliefs—i.e., let children explore freely and encourage them to find out more about what their caregivers, parents, teachers and others believe. An indepth look at your own personal beliefs will prepare you to teach children regardless of your specific role.

While exploring your *experiences* with loss and death, you'll recall that they have had both positive and negative influences on your attitudes, feelings and actions. A negative experience with death may have left you fearful, angry or cynical. As a result, you may deny your feelings, carry your anger into other, inappropriate situations or isolate yourself from people by putting down their views.

Healthy people share positive feelings, direct their hurtful feelings appropriately, and make room for those with opposing views who might present a more positive, hopeful and healthy perspective. A positive experience is one where new strengths are found. You may find this strength in new skills, new facts or stronger relationships. Only when you take a hard look into your own past can you see both the negative influences that you want to reduce and the positive influences that you want to build on.

Your past *feelings* have important lessons to teach, too. The simple act of remembering your own powerful emotions like pain or joy can remind you to be respectful of other people's feelings. It's useful to try to recall the powerful feelings aroused by death-related experiences when you're alone and are able to reflect on them. Then the strong feelings from your past will be less likely to interfere when you're trying to concentrate on a child's feelings and situation.

Being surprised by strong feelings of your own may cause you to shift the focus from the children, or frighten them with a response more intense than the situation warrants. This doesn't mean your feelings shouldn't be shared. But if you're prepared, you'll be able to handle your emotions and share them more appropriately. If you are aware of it, this emotional "spillover" is quite acceptable; it can help you be a positive role model.

How Do You Feel About Death?

The rest of this chapter offers a series of activities to help you become more comfortable with the personal and emotional aspects of loss and death. The activities are presented sequentially to allow you to investigate your history of death experiences by taking small steps. Try not to skip any activities. As you continue, keep in mind that the effort you apply to the activities will directly affect your ability to create the desired atmosphere for children. Take a break now, if you feel the need to. Find a pen and paper. Get comfortable physically, then continue getting comfortable emotionally as you take steps to find out about yourself.

As you begin this study of your personal relationship with loss and death, remember the open atmosphere concept. It is just as important for you to be open with yourself in these activities as it is for you to create an open atmosphere for children. Let the memories and feelings come as they are—some painful, some fearful, some pleasant, some confusing. You may not always have an answer, or a feeling, or an idea. That's OK too.

Consider each concept seriously. Be sincere and honest with yourself; the experience will be more helpful. Keep in mind that the way you respond today may even change; you may want to review these activities in the future to see how time and experience have affected you. Taking these first steps to self-awareness takes courage. Teachers and parents often avoid confronting their feelings regarding loss and death; but in knowing the full benefits for yourself and the children in your life, you'll find the strength you need.

Activity: Finding Death in Daily Life

Death really is a part of our daily lives. Prove it to yourself by picking up your daily newspaper—any newspaper. Scan the headlines and stories. Notice the use of death-related words even when the story doesn't relate to death (e.g., a boxing match that is "a killer," or the "deadly heat"). As you scan, keep a list of all the stories related to loss and to death. You will find elements of loss in stories about physical disabilities or rape, for example.

Take Action

Stop now, review your newspaper, and list your stories below. If you'd rather, simply use a marker and circle or highlight the death-related references you find.

_____

_____

_____

_____

Consider These Questions

1. Did you have any trouble finding loss and death-related stories or words? Why or why not?

2. Did any of the stories include references to feelings?

3. How do you feel after reading these stories? Why?

4. How did you feel about the use of death-related words in non-death stories? Is it offensive? acceptable? Why or why not?

Think About What You've Learned

You probably had no trouble finding loss- and death-related stories because they really are a part of our daily lives. And consider that the stories in the paper are only the ones an editor found noteworthy. In addition, they represent only one medium—television, radio and literature have the same degree of death-related references.

If you did have trouble finding death-related stories, it's probably because yours is a small local newspaper. Check for bigger stories and obituaries in the weekend edition or a larger city's newspaper.

These stories tend to focus mainly on facts, a reflection of the reporter's objective style that we expect in a newspaper. If you had no emotional response to a story, the situation described was probably one where you were able to remain objective. But if a story involved characters or events that reminded you of your family or friends, you probably did have an emotional response—when a story hits closer to home it's harder to remain objective.

Some stories use phrases like "I thought I'd die" or "dead tired." Such death-related phrases are common in the media and in our everyday conversation. Now that you've become aware of them, you'll notice them even more. Usually people aren't offended by these phrases—in fact, most people probably don't even think of them as related to death. The exception is when we have recently experienced a loss or death. When death touches us, all references to death in our society bring out more intense feelings.

Activity: Cultural Traditions and Religious Beliefs

The next step is to explore what your religious beliefs and cultural traditions tell you about dealing with loss and death. There are two activities to guide your exploration. The first presents a series of statements for you to consider and to decide whether you agree, are undecided, or disagree. In the second activity, you are asked to finish statements with whatever comes to mind. There are no right or wrong answers for either activity. You are simply recording your opinions.

Since we may be unable to identify our own cultural and religious beliefs because they are such an integral part of us, or because they change as our life experiences change, it is important to take time to become aware of what they are at this time. The following activity will help you clarify some of your own beliefs, help you see how your beliefs may be different from others', and note how they influence your responses to death.

Take Action—Step One

Read each statement and indicate whether you agree, are undecided, or disagree.

		Agree	Undecided	Disagree
1.	Death occurs when the brain stops working.	☐	☐	☐
2.	Funerals should be simple and dignified.	☐	☐	☐
3.	Wakes should be celebrations of life.	☐	☐	☐
4.	Children should not attend funerals.	☐	☐	☐
5.	Girls are more expressive than boys.	☐	☐	☐
6.	There is life after death.	☐	☐	☐
7.	Embalming a dead body is necessary.	☐	☐	☐
8.	It would be easier to handle death if it were sudden rather than after a prolonged illness.	☐	☐	☐

		Agree	Undecided	Disagree

9. Cremation is not an acceptable practice. ☐ ☐ ☐

10. It is important that feelings associated with grief be expressed openly. ☐ ☐ ☐

11. The funeral should reflect the dead person's personality. ☐ ☐ ☐

12. I would rather die suddenly than after a prolonged illness. ☐ ☐ ☐

13. Euthanasia is a human right. ☐ ☐ ☐

14. Laughing around a grieving person is inconsiderate. ☐ ☐ ☐

15. Visiting hours at a funeral home are depressing. ☐ ☐ ☐

16. I would rather die at home than in a hospital. ☐ ☐ ☐

17. The funeral should reflect the dead person's religion. ☐ ☐ ☐

18. People who donate organs are denying the inevitability of death. ☐ ☐ ☐

19. I hope to outlive my life partner. ☐ ☐ ☐

20. Funerals are too expensive. ☐ ☐ ☐

21. Only cemeteries that have been blessed by religious leaders are acceptable. ☐ ☐ ☐

22. The dead person should be dressed completely in white. ☐ ☐ ☐

23. Flowers and music are important parts of memorial services. ☐ ☐ ☐

24. Anyone who is interested should be allowed to participate in the memorial service. ☐ ☐ ☐

25. Vaults are a necessary part of the burial. ☐ ☐ ☐

	Agree	Undecided	Disagree

26. Relatives of the dead person must stay awake until the body is buried. ☐ ☐ ☐

27. Funeral homes are not necessary. ☐ ☐ ☐

28. Family and friends should not see the body actually being lowered into the grave. ☐ ☐ ☐

29. A funeral oration should not be given over a person who has committed suicide. ☐ ☐ ☐

30. Death-related rituals end when the body is lowered into the ground or the ashes are disposed of. ☐ ☐ ☐

Take Action—Step Two

Read the following sentence beginnings and finish the statement in your own words.

1. Religious rituals are important because

_____

_____

2. Funeral directors are

_____

_____

3. Life after death means

_____

_____

4. Memorial services should be planned and discussed before a death because

_____

_____

5. Behavior at a funeral should be

_____

_____

6. Cemeteries are

_____

_____

7. Cremated ashes should be kept

_____

_____

8. The most important factor in planning a funeral is

_____

_____

9. Visiting the family and friends is important because

_____

_____

10. A person is dead when

_____

_____

11. If I had a fatal illness, I'd want

_____

_____

Consider These Questions

1. Were your answers for both activities based on your religious training?

2. Were your answers based on your experience with death?

3. Which questions were the easiest to answer? Why do you think they were easy?

4. Which questions were the hardest to answer? Why do you think they were hard?

5. Did you feel emotional about any statements that you agreed with? disagreed with? Why or why not?

Think About What You've Learned

From the Amish custom of dressing the dead body in white, to the way crying girls are accepted while crying boys are not, cultural and religious biases influence our lives. These biases are so ingrained in us that we often react to other people's ideas with disbelief or disgust. Did you feel that way at any point while completing the previous activities? Most people do.

There is no need to adopt someone else's beliefs as your own. There is a need, however, to accept others' beliefs. An awareness of the great variety of traditions related to death will help you avoid negative responses to children's beliefs and questions. This awareness is a major step toward creating the open atmosphere children need.

Did you learn anything new about yourself through your answers? Did you learn anything new about the range of death-related beliefs and traditions? Were you surprised by some statements? Were some confusing? Did this pique your curiosity about others' views?

Activity: Your Experiences with Loss

Most parents and teachers don't believe they are adequately trained to teach about loss and death. Although you may not have any formal education in the field, this activity will prove that you do have experience with loss.

Take Action

Review this list of events or situations. Place a check mark beside the ones you have experienced at some time in your life.

Losses Related to Age

☐ childhood dreams
☐ puppy love
☐ crushes
☐ leaving school
☐ leaving home
☐ change of job
☐ loss of "youth"
☐ loss of virginity
☐ loss of health
☐ loss of physical functioning
☐ loss of mental functioning
☐ menopause
☐ retirement

Losses Related to "Everyday Living"

☐ loss of job
☐ loss of money
☐ moving
☐ change of school
☐ change of teachers
☐ loss of property
☐ loss of confidence
☐ loss of security
☐ loss of a cherished ideal
☐ loss of a long-term goal
☐ change of relationship

Obvious Losses

☐ separation
☐ divorce
☐ end of a friendship
☐ end of a relationship
☐ death of pet
☐ death of grandparent
☐ death of parent
☐ death of friend
☐ death of child
☐ death of partner

Now review the list again. This time, pause briefly at each check mark to recall any feelings associated with the events you experienced. Write down how you felt, so you can examine your feelings again later.

Consider These Questions

1. Were you surprised by the number of experiences you checked?

2. Did the feelings come easily?

3. Think about the range of feelings you experienced. Were all your feelings in the "sad" category, or were they varied?

Think About What You've Learned

Experience is a good teacher. It increases your range of facts, your awareness of what you do and don't know, and your understanding of the personal impact of the experience. Most people are surprised by how much experience they have with loss and death, and how much they remember about their experiences. Why? Because you've probably spent a lot of time and energy trying to put those "bad" times and feelings behind you, getting on with your life and trying to forget. But now you know that you don't really forget, and it's helpful to remember. Remembering and reflecting on those experiences and memories helps us learn and grow.

People often avoid memories because of the sadness involved. But you may be finding that not all your feelings were sad. On the other hand, you might not have allowed yourself to note feelings that weren't sad because you felt they were inappropriate. Feelings of relief, love and pleasure are common and appropriate responses to memories of loss- or death-related experiences. The familiar phrase "Better to have loved and lost than never to have loved at all" sums up a big part of this concept. You may have been relieved that a person didn't have to suffer any longer, or that you didn't have to watch him or her suffer. You will find more about the range of feelings associated with loss and death in Chapter 3, What Children Need to Know About Death.

What you feel is not as important as the fact that you do feel. Loss and death are natural parts of life, but they are not small and meaningless. Quite the contrary—loss of a human relationship, regardless of the cause, deserves to be treated with respect. We can learn important lessons as our lives continue beyond the loss.

Activity: Personal Experiences with Death

The next two activities will examine your personal experiences with death and use them to expand your death-education training. If you've been reading and thinking about this subject for a while you may want to take a stretch break or a deep breath. Relax and prepare to let your experiences and your feelings move you to another level of understanding death as a natural part of life.

Take Action—Step One

Take some time to reflect on the following questions. Write down your answers so you can look back at them later.

Try to remember your first experience with death.

- Who died?
- What was your relationship to the person who died?
- When did the death occur?
- How old were you at the time?
- Can you remember any of the feelings you had? What were they?

ə What were other people doing during those first few days after the death?

ə Were you allowed to help with or participate in any of the activities?

ə Did you have any questions?

ə Did someone answer your questions?

ə Did you get any "comforting"?

If yes, who comforted you?

If yes, what did they do to comfort you?

If no, what comfort would you have liked?

ə If you could, would you change anything that happened?

ə Do you still talk and reminisce about the person who died or the events around his or her death?

Take Action—Step Two

Try to remember another experience with death. Take time to reflect on the list of questions in Step One. Write down your answers again so you can look back at them later.

Consider These Questions

Review your answers to the last two activities. Compare your answers to the two different experiences with death.

1. What similarities did you find between the two experiences?

2. What differences did you find between the two experiences?

3. Why do you think differences existed?

4. What knowledge did you gain from these experiences?

5. What impact did these events have on your attitude toward death?

6. If you wanted to change some of the circumstances:

   ❧ Why do you think you wanted the changes?

   ❧ How do you think the changes would have helped?

7. What impact did others have on your experience?

8. Did you actually feel some of the same feelings while you were remembering?

9. How do you feel when you or other people talk about the death or the person who died?

10. What impact do you think your experiences will have or have had on children?

Think About What You've Learned

No two death experiences are the same. Each detail of the situation can influence your reaction. Your own age and the age of the person who died have a big impact on your experience, too. Children understand death in different ways at different ages; therefore, their reactions and memories will be different. And the death of a seven year old and the death of a 75 year old bring out different reactions among family and friends.

Relationships also influence your experiences. Your closeness with the person who died affects your response. Your closeness to other family and friends also affects you. In your experiences, did adults keep busy with rituals and tell children not to worry? This is a common situation. Adults often become so engrossed in their own grief and activities that they forget, or never become aware, that children feel sad too and need the same kind of meaningful activity to cope with the loss or death.

Often people ask questions to try to find meaning in the situation. It's our uniquely human way of trying to get our minds to understand the loss. Children are often discouraged from questioning—sometimes adults are, too. Although the potential for harm is greater when children's questions are ignored, adults can also be hurt. You may be made to feel that your questioning is morbid, nosy or inconsiderate. In reality, questioning is the way you come to accept the death and learn from the loss experience.

Sometimes death experiences lead us to make changes the next time. Death experiences make us aware that some things in life can be controlled and some cannot. You might realize that although you can't change the illness, accident and/or death, you *can* take control of some of the events surrounding the death. You can decide how the funeral will take place, can let yourself cry more, can keep yourself busier, or can ask for the comfort you need. Any action you take will balance, however slightly, your loss of control over the death.

When you thought about what would make you feel better, did you think about what comfort means to you? Did you think about how to comfort someone else? Comforting comes in many forms, but it usually involves interaction with other human beings. You may also need time alone, but not *only* time alone. Human beings need to know that other human beings understand the depth of their feelings. Sharing your feelings is a primary source of comfort. It can be fulfilled by friends, family, and/or religion. Seek comfort in whatever ways make *you* feel stronger.

Some people seek comfort in memories of the one who died. They enjoy telling and hearing stories about him or her and about the events surrounding the death. If this comforts you, allow it to continue. If these stories seem hurtful or pointless to you, think of it this way: When the person no longer exists in body, what do you have left? The memories! You have control of the memories. Do you really want to give them away? Or do you want to share them and let them comfort you? Memories are helpful and often pleasant as a part of your life. Remembering the past is healthy when it helps you live for the present and plan for the future.

As you remembered your experiences, some of your feelings and thoughts may have been unique, while others may have been common human responses. Some of your feelings and thoughts may have been painful and difficult, while others may have been pleasant. Still others may have been confusing and worrisome. The important lesson is to know your uniqueness even while knowing you are not alone in your reactions. Enjoy and build on the positive feelings while respecting and learning from the difficult ones. Leave your mind open for answers to the confusing questions—time and experience still may have lessons to offer.

Activity: Thinking About Your Own Death

This last step in the self-exploration process is the most personal activity. You will be asked to think about your own death. Each of the previous steps has prepared you for this last activity. You know how to balance yourself by looking at the difficult feelings as lessons and using the positive feelings for comfort. As you completed the other activities, you've probably made some mental notes already about things you liked and didn't like. Now is the time to give some order to those notes and plan your own memorial events.

Take Action

Think about your own memorial service and burial rituals using the following statements. Select one of the answers given, or write your own answer for each blank.

1. I want a *big/small/*_____ funeral.

2. I hope that people at my funeral are *happy/sad/* _____.

3. I want music to be *quiet/religious/upbeat/*_____.

4. I want the service to be *traditional/a unique reflection of me/*
    _____.

5. The service should be *religious/nonreligious*_____.

6. The service should be *private/public/* _____.

7. I want the service to *be directed by professionals/include my
    family and friends/*_____.

8. I want the decorations to be *colorful/extravagant/plain/simple/*
    _____.

9. I want people to make memorials by giving *flowers/donations to
    family/donations to charity/* _____.

10. I would like to be *buried/cremated/* _____.

11. If buried, I want *an airtight casket and vault/a simple wooden
    coffin/*_____.

12. If cremated, I want my ashes to be *kept in a mausoleum/buried/
    scattered/kept with my family/*_____.

13. Describe any other details about your death and the related rituals
    (e.g., epitaph, tombstone, obituary, procession to cemetery, family
    involvement, how you want to be remembered, etc.).

    _____

    _____

    _____

    _____

    _____

    _____

    _____

    _____

Consider These Questions

- ❧ How did you feel about making decisions and writing about your own death?

- ❧ Were some parts harder than others? If so, why?

- ❧ Did you surprise yourself with any answers?

- ❧ Did you describe a traditional or nontraditional service?

- ❧ How do you think your family and friends would react to your choices?

- ❧ Would you consider sharing this information with family? with friends?

Think About What You've Learned

Were you prepared for this step? Some people believe that you are never prepared to accept losses or your own death. Do you agree? Or did this chapter help you see the value of exploring your beliefs and feelings? Whether you were able to complete this activity or not, don't try to compare yourself with anyone else. You've probably gone as far as you can for now.

The next time you review the chapter you may decide to explore further. You are in the process of exploring your life, loss and death experiences, and learning from them. Taking these steps toward self-awareness and acceptance of death as part of life often makes our lives fuller. How do you feel about this?

Did your responses surprise you? Why? Was it because you were able to handle the thought of your own death better than you thought you could? Was it because you are more untraditional than you thought you were? Maybe you realized that your religion is more important to you than you thought. Or you realized that you aren't afraid of dying. Are you concerned about how your death will affect your family and friends?

If you're aware of being surprised, for whatever reasons, congratulate yourself on your honesty and on creating an open atmosphere in which to explore your personal attitudes toward death. When you're ready, you may want to take time to share your experiences with friends and family. Even if they're not open to discussing death, you can let them know that you're considering these issues.

The Next Step

These activities have brought you through to self-discovery in stages, introducing increasingly personal and emotional questions at each level. When you take small steps like this, you're able to handle bigger concepts. Your experience here can serve as a guide when you're working with children. As you implement the activities for children in this book, you'll notice that they are presented in small stages. As teacher, parent or caregiver, you'll decide where to start and how fast and how far the children can go in their exploration of loss and death.

Now that you have examined how you relate to loss and death, you need to know how children relate to death. What does "sad" mean to a three year old? To a six year old? To a ten year old? The next chapter, How Children Learn About Death, describes the growth and development of children's ability to think in different ways. As the way they think changes and grows, their ability to understand death expands. Exploring loss and death from a child's perspective is the next step in preparing to educate children about death.

Chapter 2

How Children Learn About Death

Whether children are aware of it or not, loss and death are part of their lives. Children watch television, read or hear stories, watch adults grieve, overhear hushed voices, change homes, change parents, change schools, hear prayers, see funeral processions, step on spiders, lose a special teddy bear, and "die" for a chocolate ice-cream cone. These experiences may come from the media, from customs and language in their culture, or from their religious training. Regardless of the source, messages are being sent and children are receiving them.

Depending on the age of the child at the time of the experience, these messages will vary. The younger the child, the fuzzier the message, leaving room for different interpretations. The older the child, the clearer the message. Children learn about death in small steps as their experiences and their abilities to think expand. Your job is to discern what your children already know and what they are capable of learning. When you can do this, you'll be able to make the messages about death and loss clearer and more meaningful.

You needn't have all the answers. You just have to help the children with their next steps. At some point, you may even be learning together. That's one of the joys of the open atmosphere being promoted here: you have the freedom to say, "I don't know, but let's find out together."

Stages of Understanding

In general, young children understand the concrete or physical world first. As they get older, they learn to reason and think about things they can't see or touch. The growth in their abilities occurs in predictable stages well established by child psychologists, based on a child's readiness to understand new information. A child's readiness to move on depends on how fully the current stage is explored.

And children move through the developmental stages at different rates depending on the intensity of their experiences, the amount of adult guidance they receive, and the innate abilities of each child. Because of these individual differences, specific ages associated with each stage are just reference points. The *sequence* of stages is what is important—not specific ages.

Children follow these predictable stages in developing their understanding of loss and death just as they do with other subjects. When they first acknowledge death they see it as *reversible, avoidable* and *impersonal.* By the time they are nine or ten they see death as *final, inevitable* and *personal.* The following sections will define these terms and describe how children move through four typical developmental stages: under age three, ages three through five, ages six through eight, and age nine and over.

Stage One: Under Age Three

Children in stage one have limited verbal abilities, which makes them a difficult group to study. As a result, there are varied opinions and little research to confirm what children understand at this stage. We can make some logical assumptions however.

Some researchers (Furman, 1978; Wenestam and Wass, 1987) have studied children under three and found reactions and understanding related to death. We must acknowledge that these responses are *possible;* whether or not they are typical is less important.

It is also logical that if children have individual differences in ability, adult guidance, and degree of experience; then it would be possible for some two year olds to understand death and react to it. For example, an observant parent or teacher of a bright one or two year old may notice a behavior change when something or someone important in the child's life is missing.

The fact that very young children don't use words the way older children and adults do does not mean they don't experience similar feelings of loss. Be careful not to extend the assumption to include all children under three years old—just the possibility for some of them.

Stage Two: Ages Three Through Five

Four developmental characteristics affect children's understanding of death during this stage: time, egocentrism, animism and magical thinking.

At this stage, children have a limited concept of the first characteristic—*time*. Although they may be learning about yesterday and tomorrow, anything longer than that is quite unreal to them. As a result, the child is unable to see death as final. Instead, death is commonly viewed as temporary. For example, "Grandma is dead today, but she'll be back next week."

A second characteristic of this stage is the inability to see the world from someone else's perspective—*egocentrism*. This allows children to completely disregard a death that doesn't come close enough to touch their world directly. It is not seen as personal. So, at this stage, children often surprise adults with what appears to be a matter-of-fact, calm acceptance of death. The child may be accepting the words, but the words don't have any real meaning.

On the other hand, as a result of being egocentric, preschool children may believe that a loss or death is a result or consequence of their own actions. This response presents one of the greatest challenges for parents, teachers and caregivers when talking to children about death. If any child expresses a sense of *responsibility* for a loss or for a natural or accidental death, he or she *must* be reassured that this is not so. This appears to contradict the earlier discussion about developing an open atmosphere with an accepting attitude, but accepting a child's feelings of responsibility for a death is clearly harmful and inappropriate.

Animism, the third characteristic of this stage, refers to the tendency to believe that inanimate objects such as rocks and blankets are alive. Children don't often make the distinction between animate and inanimate objects. Thus they cannot understand the physical difference between life and death. Death appears to be just a different state, like hungry or tired, not the absence of life. This perspective also accounts for some children's ability to respond calmly. They don't understand the full meaning of death that typically causes adult responses.

Finally, the child in stage two engages in *magical thinking*. Children believe that people and objects have power to make other people and objects do things. For example, children may conclude that if they never break another house rule, their divorced parents will get back together. Or if the child gives Granddad a lucky rabbit's foot, then Granddad won't die. A resourceful child will use this magical thinking to "fix it," or find a solution with a happy ending. Magical thinking allows a child to see death as reversible and avoidable.

Stage Three: Ages Six Through Eight

This period is a major transitional stage for children. Initially they are learning to see death as final and then inevitable for all living things, *except* themselves. By the end of this stage they may also understand that death is *personal*. Because there is such a drastic change of view during this stage, you will see greater differences between individual children—and even within one child.

Children experience great conflict as they learn the biological fact of death's inevitability, yet still hold onto the magic of "not me." Their early views of death give way as they develop an understanding of the depth of loss. Although the words we use to describe our adult view of death seem simple, for children to understand fully the concepts of *final, inevitable* and *personal* they must take some huge steps.

During this third developmental stage children are very interested in death, especially physical details. They will have a million questions for a concerned and available adult. They want to know about the causes of death, the rituals associated with death and the physical aspects like coffins, tombstones and funeral homes. As these concepts become clearer, many children in this stage begin questioning what happens after death.

Stage Four: Age Nine and Over

Somewhere around age nine or ten most children reach an adult-like understanding of death. They understand that death is *final, inevitable* and *personal.* They can define death in medical and biological terms and can think about death in an abstract manner. At this time, children can begin to grasp the metaphors and similes often used in discussions of death—the way, for example, that people "live on in our memories" or are "given back to the earth to nurture new growth."

Although children in this stage may have the mental ability to understand the facts related to death, they may still be limited in their experiences with death and their ability to cope with the emotions involved. No one outgrows the need for emotional support at a time of loss or death.

Remember that the ages given here are just reference points for developmental stages. Factors other than age affect when a child will move into the next stage. A child's personal abilities, adult guidance, and the number and intensity of loss and death experiences were mentioned earlier. The following sections provide details about the influences of media, culture and religion. Regardless of the specific ages at which children develop death concepts, it is critical to understand that their concepts of death become increasingly more detailed and factual over time.

Lessons in the Media

Children who watch television and movies and read books are filing away important bits of information about loss and death. Although all these media sources include information about death, it is not their main purpose to teach about death. That's our job as teachers and parents. But children are learning from the media anyway.

Unfortunately, such media often give inaccurate, inconsistent or confusing information that reinforces children's misconceptions. Parents and teachers must learn to work with the media messages. To use the messages to help children develop a healthy understanding of loss and death, you must understand how media messages affect them.

Television and Movies

Think about what children see on television. A news anchor calmly comments on the number of people killed in a war on the other side of the world. A reporter at the scene emotionally describes gruesome details of a fiery crash. A cartoon character gets flattened by a steam roller, and after a brief pause and a frown gets up to continue a chase. A character in a weekly mystery series gets killed, only to show up the next week on a comedy show on another network. In movies the dead person sometimes is portrayed as someone horrible who "deserved to die" or elderly and "ready to die."

Do you think a child might wonder why those people were killed, or why the news anchor didn't seem to care about the dead people? Could children be frightened by details of a crash? Could they be interested in the details without any accompanying emotions? Using their imaginations, could children decide that the cartoon character got up because he was stronger than the steam roller or that the man who died on the mystery show got better because he wanted to be on the comedy show next week?

Do some people really deserve to die? Think about our language. If an elderly person can be "ready to die," is that what the high school basketball star meant when he said he was ready to die when his team lost the game? Are you confused? Think how confused children must be.

Now think about how children respond to these media images. Do they accept them? Do they ignore them? Do they worry about them? Do they fill in the gaps in their understanding with their own imaginings? Any of these responses are possible.

How do you know what your children are thinking? First, you need to know what they're watching. The best way to know what children are watching is to watch with them. Then use the open atmosphere you've created to help children understand their experiences. If they don't ask questions about what the story means, you can ask questions about what they're thinking or feeling. This is your chance to set the record straight. You can correct any inaccurate information and confusing misconceptions.

If you are a teacher you'll have less opportunity to watch TV with the children. But you can still ask questions about what they're seeing. As you begin a death education lesson you can ask if they've seen any examples of your lesson concept on television. Was it in a movie or on the news—i.e., fact or fiction? You can ask for facts, feelings or other characters' responses, depending on your lesson focus. If an especially disturbing happening in your community is being shown or discussed on TV, you can begin the next day at school with "How many of you heard about...? What do you think about it?" You can set the record straight, clarifying facts as necessary. Chapter 5, Using Planned Learning Activities, includes an example of how to use media in teaching.

Literature

Children's literature also includes references to death, which can have an influence on children's perceptions. Because books are a big part of many children's lives, adults need to know how to identify positive approaches and use children's literature appropriately. When a child chooses a book with a negative approach, like depicting a grieving child being left alone with no adult comforter, you need to understand the impact this might have and discuss the child's fears. If you can allay the fears honestly, do that as well.

When you're choosing a book, look for those with positive approaches. Children's books usually present only a small part of a death-related experience. Handling small steps at a time is a good way to deal with death education. Chapters 5 and 7 offer more help with using children's literature. The Feelings in Children's Literature activity in Chapter 5 suggests ways to use literature, and Chapter 7 recommends specific children's books with positive approaches and identifies the important death concepts illustrated in each book.

As you discuss the content of television, newspapers, radio and literature that children are exposed to, you will have many opportunities to teach about death. We're not suggesting that you turn every activity into a structured learning experience. But understanding the influence of these materials and how to use them can help when you need to clarify or initiate a conversation about loss or death.

Lessons from the Culture

In our culture, loss and death are thought of as significant human concerns. But do all segments of our culture see them exactly the same way? Probably not. For example, social and economic factors affect the time available for grief, the money available for memorials, the exposure to loss and death, and thus the overall attitudes about how to deal with loss and death.

Time and Attention

We know that grieving for any loss or death takes time and attention. Some children learn that adults take time off work to make arrangements, deal with their feelings, share special time with family and friends, maybe even take a family vacation to ease the tensions. Others may learn that grief must be scheduled around work time—in the evenings and weekends. Business and physical arrangements, such as finding a new home, enrolling children in new schools, or planning a funeral, may come first, with adult coping next, and children getting the limited time left over, if any. Time becomes a commodity, even a luxury, having a direct impact on the way children experience loss and death. Children who receive different amounts of time and attention may not see the same picture when coping with loss and death.

The Memorial Service

Children don't all get the same picture when attending a memorial service, either. The memorial service may be affected by the amount of money available from family, friends or other sources such as insurance. There are different grades of funeral homes to choose from, just as we have different grades of department stores for our shopping. If you use a funeral home, your choice determines the extravagance or simplicity of the physical setting and sometimes the amount of personal care you receive from the funeral director and staff.

Many other choices you make depend on what you can afford. For example, sometimes evening hours for visitation and/or funerals are more expensive than daytime hours. If you request that memorial donations be sent to the family or to favorite charities, or if friends and family have a low income level, there may be fewer flowers for decorations. These variations make children's experiences very different. As a result, their picture or perception of what is "right" or "normal" may vary too.

Variations in Experience

The degree of exposure to loss and death also creates different pictures for children in different social and economic groups. Some children may often have to move into new homes, have to adjust to leaving old friends and making new ones—even adjust to new parents. Some might experience gang wars and violent, meaningless deaths.

At the other extreme are children who may live in one neighborhood with few home changes and keep the same friends and parents through the years. They might experience only news reports of deaths of strangers, and natural deaths of aging or seriously ill pets and loved ones.

Such extreme variations in experience have a profound effect on a child's understanding of death. When children change homes frequently they may learn just to be adaptable. And when they have difficulty isolating a day when violence and loss are not involved, they may learn to ignore death or pretend it isn't real. They may wear themselves down fighting for change or trying to make sense of the experiences, or they may become angry and violent.

Lessons learned when children's home lives are stable, supportive and nonviolent are quite different. Children are able to confront the difficulties in their lives, explore them freely and learn from them. These positive experiences help children balance painful experiences related to loss and death. Such children are capable of seeing loss and death as a natural part of life.

Children receive messages from their community too. The ethnic background of their neighbors and their geographic location produce different views of life and death. A child from an urban area where cemeteries are crowded and surrounded closely with other buildings would have a a very different idea of burial than a child from a rural western area where cemeteries are sprawled in open country. A child who grows up observing loud, joyful Irish Catholic wakes will have a different expectation than a child who observes a typically somber German Protestant visitation.

Cultural messages are not as obvious as media messages, although their influences are as strong. When a child's culture is the same as your own it is difficult to be objective enough to identify the messages. Our culture is so much a part of us that separating ourselves from it is a challenge. But we need to try. Think about some of the death-related customs of our culture and the language we use to describe loss and death.

Some people believe in putting a death behind them as quickly and quietly as possible, while others believe that open mourning is helpful. Individuals from these two backgrounds will find it difficult to talk to each other. The quiet person may feel that being asked about the deceased is impolite because it's a personal matter, while the open person may feel that the quiet person is unfeeling if the death is not asked about.

The quiet, extremely private individual may be uncomfortable discussing the funeral details or the death, and end up saying things like "I was sorry to hear about your mother's passing. I hope all the arrangements worked out all right." If this is how you would talk, it probably seems perfectly acceptable. But some people might respond with thoughts or words like "Why can't you ask me about the casket I picked out?" or "She didn't 'pass' anything—she died, and I miss her."

Some of the lessons children learn about loss and death are the same throughout most social and economic groups. Some of the broad influences on children's perceptions are our mobile society, a depersonalization of death, and an unwillingness to speak about death directly. While all three aspects of our culture play a part in developing a child's view, the way we hide death with indirect language is the most critical. Fortunately, it is also the area where caring adults can make the most difference.

Our Mobile Society

The mobile society and the depersonalization of death have overlapping influences on children. Because people move around so much, many children must get used to learning new school rules, making new friends and saying goodbye to what's familiar. While this might improve the adaptability of some children, for others it might create a barrier to developing meaningful relationships.

In addition, our mobile society causes children to be more isolated from older generations of their families and thus more isolated from the natural deaths of those generations. This means that when children experience death it is more likely to be in a hospital or on television than in their homes. Death thus seems less personal.

Video Games

Another example of depersonalization comes from an activity that almost all children are exposed to—video games. When a video game is over, children often say, "I died." The object of many video games is to "kill" other characters or objects on the screen. Having more than one life for your character or earning additional lives throughout the course of the game is common. Based on the earlier discussion of children's stages in understanding, you can see how the video game experience might feed into the inability to distinguish between animate and inanimate objects.

Along with some cartoons, comic strips and movies, video games can foster a child's belief that death is temporary. Even in the advanced stage of understanding, video games are likely to create a depersonalization or desensitization toward death. Being aware of these possibilities can help you see when a child needs your help in making distinctions between real death and figurative language.

Indirect Language

The way adults make references to death also influences the development of the child's view. When adults use symbolic or indirect language to talk about death they may be giving a child misleading or confusing information. Unnecessary fears may be aroused in the child.

Consider the perspective of young children in the following examples: A child develops the flu two days after being told that a close relative died because he was "sick." A second child is told that a deceased grandparent "went away" months or even years earlier. Could this child be angry about being left without a goodbye? What if the parent has to "go away" on a business trip?

Another child is told that someone who has died is "asleep" or "on a journey." What response would be expected from this child at bedtime or vacation time? Even if well intended, indirect or symbolic language can send harmful messages.

The positive side is that adults *can* learn to speak openly and directly with children about death. Chapters 3 and 4 offer some suggestions for eliminating indirect language from your conversations with children about death.

Lessons from Religion

Unlike the varied and unplanned messages from media and culture, messages from religion are presented with the purpose of teaching specific beliefs. Many religious groups require certain beliefs and rituals related to death. This section discusses some examples of the different ways religions approach life after death, funeral and memorial services, and burial and mourning rituals.

Most religions have in common a belief in life after death. The differences are found in the various definitions of this life after death. For some, life after death means that the spirit or soul lives on in heaven, hell or purgatory. Others believe in reincarnation, where the spirit or soul is physically reborn in another life form. Still others believe that the spirit lives on in the human interactions, or memories, of the surviving loved ones; or that it lives on in the earth as part of the natural cycle of decomposed matter nourishing new life.

Most religions have a common belief that some type of memorial service is an important part of mourning the death of a loved one. The details of the services can vary. In some religions, the funeral service must be directed by a leader of the church. Other religions encourage, and some require, that those close to the one who has died participate in the service. Many churches are unconcerned about the specific location of the service. Some do not allow involvement of a funeral home.

Some religions require a somber attitude, without music or flowers. Many religions have no rules about decorations, but it may be commonly accepted that the more flowers the greater the tribute to the deceased. When the church teachings don't specify the atmosphere or behavior expected, you may see anything from a quiet, somber service to a loud celebration.

For some religions, no differences occur in the funeral when suicide is the cause of death. Other religions have strict rules against a formal religious funeral for a person who has committed suicide.

The most commonly accepted way of dealing with the dead body is burial. Cremation is another alternative which is accepted by many religions, not accepted by some religions, and preferred by a few. When burial is chosen, some religions require that the cemetery be one which has been blessed by a church dignitary. Most religions allow individual choice regarding whether burial is in the ground or in a mausoleum.

Viewing the dead body is often a matter of choice, but in some religions it is allowed only for the family. A few religions expect that family members will clean and care for the dead body. Some religions require that the body be dressed in all white. Some require that family members stay awake from the time of death until the time of burial.

❧ ❧ ❧

Children learn facts and attitudes as they develop their understanding of death. The facts are learned in stages as their minds expand and they are able to think in new ways. Regardless of their mental abilities, children are taking in messages at all ages from media, culture and religion. The degree of death-related experiences and adult guidance influences how they understand the messages and how quickly they move through the stages toward an adult understanding of death.

Because children see different social and cultural pictures based on their individual experiences with death, their perceptions of what is "right" or "normal" are very different too. In most cases they are adopting the attitudes of the adults in their lives who are continuing a particular cultural perspective.

Although changes occur in cultural perspectives, it takes a long time for a new view to become accepted. While death is still a taboo topic for many, the children in your lives will be experiencing a change in cultural perspective when you help them to see loss and death as natural parts of life—important parts of life that can be shared growing experiences.

Chapter 3

What Children Need to Know About Death

There are two general approaches to teaching about loss and death. Sometimes you will introduce the topic of loss and death through a planned series of learning activities. Or children may introduce the topic, at home or at school, as a result of something they saw on television, something they heard about, or a current loss or death experience. Planned death education and activities to explore current death experiences are both critical for a well-rounded, healthy learning experience (Elkind, 1977; Ordal, 1980; Wass and Corr, 1982).

Whichever approach you're using, there are four specific topic areas to be considered—not all at one time, but in individual steps. You'll determine which topic area, or combination of areas, is most relevant and important for the specific situation. All four areas have to be covered eventually; all steps need to be taken as children are able to understand the concepts and cope with the feelings, based on the developmental stages discussed in Chapter 2.

This chapter provides background information to help you understand the four topic areas:

- teaching facts
- sharing feelings
- sharing beliefs
- teaching coping skills

Teaching Facts

Learning facts is one step children need to take in their quest to understand loss and death in their lives. What do they need to know about loss and death? How do we, as concerned yet uncertain adults, approach the subject when the guidelines from experts aren't clear-cut? How do we explain difficult concepts without causing fear, emotional pain, confusion or mistrust? Although many of the answers to these questions depend on a child's readiness to understand facts, other guide-lines can be applied more generally.

Identify the Level of Understanding

First, look for clues that will identify children's level of understanding (as described in Chapter 2). Accumulated history and current daily experiences both tell much about children. Did the children see a funeral procession when they were riding the bus home from school yesterday? Did they see a gruesome murder being discussed on the evening news? How are they reacting? How do they describe the event? What questions do they ask?

If they announce the event with little emotion and quickly go on to the next activity, they may be in the three-through-five stage. If they describe great detail and ask questions about physical aspects, they may be in the six-through-eight stage. If they contemplate what their own funeral procession might look like, they are probably in the nine-and-over stage.

If you pay attention to the language they use, you can find clues to children's level of understanding and the meaning of their words. When possible, use these same words to clarify terms and concepts.

Once you've identified the level of understanding, you can move on to the specific facts you want to teach. The facts don't change for different children, but the amount of information, the degree of detail and the language used will vary with the developmental stage of the children.

Tell the Truth

Adults know that half-truths and incorrect information lead to fear, misunderstanding and mistrust. Think about someone who has lied to you. Did you trust the person after that? Probably not! The same thing is true of children. If you lie to them about death, they will be less trusting of you in the future.

For children, lack of trust in the significant adults in their lives has serious consequences. If children realize that they can't trust the information you're giving them about loss and death, they are likely to conclude that they can't trust *any* information you give them. Maybe it's *not* really important to look both ways before you cross the street!

Without the help of an honest adult interpreter of their loss-related experiences, children are less likely to benefit from those experiences. Instead, they may imagine their own version of truth—a version often more frightening than the actual truth.

Children deserve to know the truth, but as their interpreter you have to decide how much they're able to understand. Resist the urge to use these limits to justify shielding them from reality. Respect the strength of their emotions and their ability to understand. Then give them direct, honest answers at the highest level you believe they will understand.

As you strive to determine what children are able to accept and understand, these questions might help:

- What do I see as the real question from the child's point of view?

- How much information and what degree of detail should be presented?

- How can I present the information in a matter-of-fact, objective manner?

As you consider your answers to these questions, remember the developmental stages of children discussed in Chapter 2.

Think Like a Child

When reacting to children's questions and comments based on their own interpretation, adults may jump to conclusions far beyond the child's understanding. If a five year old asks, "What happens when a person dies?" the child may simply want to know that the body is taken to a funeral home where it is put in a casket to be buried. If an adult begins a discussion of heaven and hell, children may jump to frightening conclusions. For example, how easily a child might think, "Since I don't know how to fly to heaven, I will have to go to that bad place—hell." To avoid this unnecessary trauma and fear, remember the developmental abilities of children at different stages and try to look at things from their point of view.

This may seem a daunting responsibility! What if you don't give the right answers, aimed at the proper level of understanding? What if your answer is too long or too involved? These fears are natural, but trust your skills as parent or teacher. You've probably been communicating with children for years. You know that any time you discuss something, you follow up by looking for clues telling you the children understood. Use those same skills and clues when talking about loss and death.

Ask questions. Observe expressions and behavior. Know that some children will continue to ask questions until they feel confident in their understanding. If they don't, you can ask *them* questions. Their answers to your questions will help you decide whether they have understood your message. If they withdraw or act out, consider whether your message has prompted this behavior. Then be prepared to clarify. Remember, there are no "right" answers. No one knows exactly what to say, or when. Trust your heart, your intuition and your relationship with the children.

Avoid Judgment

Although there are no right answers, there *is* a right attitude. When talking to children about loss and death it's important to avoid judgment. It's important to be matter of fact, and to be objective when you present the facts. *Objective* doesn't mean "without feeling." Someone who is objective does not indulge in approval or disapproval.

Having the right attitude extends even to what might be considered a concrete concept—biological death. Does death occur when the brain stops, when the heart stops, or when the lungs stop—or when all three stop? There is no universally "right" answer; it depends on your beliefs. But acknowledging that all these views exist is the right *attitude*.

When we move into the more subjective aspects of rituals, feelings and beliefs, presenting the range of ideas is more important than judging which is correct. Parents are free to let children know what they themselves believe. Teachers, however, need to emphasize that individual variations exist and are determined by individual beliefs. Right or wrong, approval or judgment, should not be a part of the lesson.

Use Appropriate Language

Along with appropriate facts and attitude, consider appropriate language. (Refer to the table in Chapter 4 for suggestions on direct language.) Remember that when you try to shield a child from the painful details surrounding loss and death by substituting less direct words, you may unwittingly create fear or confusion. If death is being "asleep," then who would want to sleep? If death is a "trip to heaven," then why can't I go, too? Once you become more comfortable discussing loss and death, you'll be able to resist the urge to use these euphemisms.

When you're working with younger children, resist metaphors too. Metaphors are too abstract for young children to understand. In an attempt to make sense of your metaphor, they may put the message into their own concrete terms. If a buried pet is said to be nourishment for flowers that will grow in the spring, a child's interpretation might be that the pet comes back to life and waters the plants, or that the buried pet magically changes form and becomes a flower. Children given metaphors may end up with confusing thoughts that are difficult to overcome as they continue their climb to higher levels of understanding.

Sharing Feelings

How do children feel about loss and death? What makes them feel that way? How can you help them explore, express and understand those feelings? The answers to these questions may help you develop a positive approach to helping children explore their feelings related to loss and death.

Acknowledge, Explore and Accept Feelings

As parents and teachers, we must approach helping children explore feelings by developing a thorough respect for each child's reactions and emotions. Focus on the fact that children *do* experience loss and grief. Believe that their feelings are as strong to them as ours are to us. This respect and compassion for children's views of life is the foundation of an ability to acknowledge, explore, accept and discuss children's feelings.

If you don't know about acknowledging, here's how it works. A child says, "I'm so sad!" or he or she withdraws from an activity normally considered fun and interesting. Adults often respond by trying to "make it all better" or even by ignoring the child's feeling for fear of handling it poorly or getting too involved. Some adults may not even recognize the sadness.

The thing to do is to *acknowledge the child's feelings.* You can say, "I can see [or hear] how sad you are. I get sad, too. It's OK to be sad." Then depending on the child and the situation, you can lead into a discussion of related questions: "Why do you [we] feel sad? What do you [we] do when you [we] feel sad? What makes you [us] feel better when you're [we're] sad?"

When you ignore or "take over" a child's feelings, you reduce the child's power to handle feelings. The unspoken message is that "you can't handle this bad feeling, so I'll handle it for you." Your intentions may be good, but children need the chance to practice and express their feelings. With especially strong feelings like those associated with loss and grief, practice doesn't make perfect, either. But practice does help us learn important life lessons—"Life goes on," "I can handle this," "It won't last forever," and other attitudes that help people cope with difficult situations.

When you ignore a child's feelings, you lower the child's self-esteem. Not acknowledging the feelings sends a message that children interpret in different—mostly harmful—ways. A child might conclude: "What I feel isn't important enough to comment about." Or, "What I feel is wrong." Or "What I feel is so scary that even the grownups don't want to think about it." These messages arouse feelings that can be more confusing, painful or frightening than the initial response to loss and death.

By acknowledging the child's feelings you send these messages: "Your feelings are important. Your feelings are OK. Your feelings can be handled." And "You're important to me." Given these supportive messages, children are empowered to explore their feelings. Remember, we can't learn to cope with feelings until we have fully explored them. To learn from feelings, we have to experience them.

Once children's feelings are acknowledged, children and adults are free to explore them together. And sharing with adults helps children practice expressing their feelings. When children (and adults) learn to put their feelings into words and actions, a new area of support is opened. Help and/or comfort can be asked for.

Sometimes just the act of sharing the feeling spreads the weight of the sadness between the child and adult. Don't you feel better when you know someone else knows how you feel, and cares about how you feel? When children feel this kind of support and understanding, they are able to get through the immediate situation and break through to the other side—they remember that there are good feelings in their lives too. Then comes the awakening that they really can bear the difficult problems and feelings in their lives. Painful feelings don't last forever; life does go on.

Create an Open Atmosphere

An "open atmosphere" is particularly important here. To help children explore feelings related to loss and death, create an environment where children's feelings are accepted, where both adult and child feelings are discussed openly, and where children are comforted.

Remember, you must be accepting and comfortable with your own feelings before you can provide the open atmosphere children need. If you evaluate or judge children's feelings, you are putting the children in a no-win situation. If they disagree with you, they may feel guilty or conclude that their own feelings are wrong—maybe even bad.

Frequently adults try to interpret children's words and meanings. It is important to not interpret but to simply accept children's feelings at face value. There are no right ways for adults to feel when grieving, and there are no right ways for children to feel when grieving. (Remember that there is one exception to this rule: When children express any sense of responsibility for a natural loss or death they must be reassured "It's not your fault!")

Sharing your feelings with children is almost as important as encouraging them to share their feelings with you. While their feelings remain the focus of your sharing, telling them how you feel may open up new ideas or help them accept their own feelings more readily. If someone they admire—like you—feels the same way as they do, it must be OK. If someone they admire—like you—feels differently, it gives them some new ways to look at things (when they're able).

Be a Role Model

This is an important opportunity to role-model for children. They can watch you express feelings, agree with feelings, or disagree with but respect the feelings of others. Think about it: Did you have a role model for these feelings as a child? If you had had one, would you be better at expressing your feelings and accepting those of others?

So far, we've discussed words as the primary way of communicating support, acceptance and encouragement. While words truly are powerful comforters, there are times when touch can be even more powerful. Degree and type of touch depends on the relationship between you and the child.

Obviously parents will be more physically involved with their children than teachers. But there may be times, at home or at school, when physical comfort is needed. A touch, a hug or a knowing smile can all have a profound effect on children. When you know a child is troubled or upset but you can't put the feelings into words, a touch can communicate your compassion. We all know that a picture is worth a thousand words. When dealing with loss and death, sometimes a touch can be worth a thousand words as well.

Sharing Beliefs

Sharing beliefs is another important area for parents and teachers to include in their death education plans. Sharing beliefs about loss and death is much like sharing feelings. There is a great range of different beliefs to be acknowledged, respected, explored, accepted and discussed. Some are based in religion, others come from socially accepted practices or norms. How do you deal with diversity and still provide lessons that children can understand?

The same basic guidelines also work here. You share yourself and your viewpoints; you maintain an open, welcome atmosphere; and you resist the urge to shield children from painful parts of life.

Different Roles of Parents and Teachers

Sharing beliefs is an area where parents and teachers may find the greatest differences between their roles. Feelings and facts are almost universal, and acceptance of other viewpoints is not usually threatening or distasteful. With personal beliefs, however, parents may focus on presenting the specific beliefs of the family and/or their religion while teachers must present the variety of beliefs held within the school district, community, country or world without endorsing any particular belief.

Teachers usually would not choose to present only one personal or religious view. Teachers have the responsibility to present a balanced view, one showing the range of different beliefs. If a teacher is not objective in this area, students may be confused or angry because their own cultures are not recognized in the classroom.

In contrast, parents or caregivers do explain their personal religious and cultural beliefs to their children. Although parents might adopt a teacher's focus by presenting a variety of beliefs and urging their children to accept others' beliefs even when they disagree, they are likely to end by encouraging their children to adopt beliefs similar to their own. When children are allowed to choose their own beliefs, caregivers should share the many possibilities with them so that they can understand the choices.

Small Steps, Open Atmosphere

A child's beliefs need to be explored in small steps—and in an open atmosphere. When you make loss and death a natural, comfortable topic in your home or classroom, you are showing that loss is a part of life. If you whisper or fidget nervously when children bring up the subject, they will sense that you are uncomfortable discussing loss and death and will stop asking questions.

When you are natural in your voice and mannerisms, children will know that it's OK to ask "What is heaven?" and "Why did the minister say Uncle Joe had gone to a better place?" They will feel free to express their theories: "I think when a person dies their body is gone except for their brain. I think their brain goes into another person's brain and then the living person knows everything that the dead person knew. That's why some people are smarter than others."

Just as with denying children's feelings, denying their beliefs reduces their self-esteem and cuts off their opportunity to practice expressing and getting feedback on their thoughts—clearly obstacles to growing and developing positively. Allowing children to explore and express their beliefs and learn from their exploration tells them they can come to you with their ideas. You are then given the opportunity to clarify or simply acknowledge their concepts as needed.

Acknowledge the Importance of Death

When adults attempt to shield children from the difficult situations and feelings in life, they often cause the children to believe that these situations are unimportant, that the related feelings are unimportant, and—worst of all—that the children themselves are unimportant.

Loss and death *are* important parts of life. When a big brother goes away to college or simply doesn't spend time with a little brother anymore, the little brother may experience a severe loss. When someone we love moves away or dies, we don't want children to believe that it's not important enough to discuss. We don't want them to think that if they move away or die, we won't miss them.

Relationships with friends and loved ones are crucial to our well-being. Loss of these relationships through whatever means affects us greatly. We need to acknowledge and experience all the feelings associated with loss—feel bad, even get mad—if we are to learn how to move beyond the difficult times and become stronger individuals. Our experiences of grief and loss develop the beliefs that help us cope with life experiences.

Teaching Coping Skills

The fourth area for teaching about loss and death is coping skills. Remember two key elements when providing guidance in this area: involvement and memories. These are the same coping mechanisms adults find helpful. Because children experience similar feelings of grief, they, too, benefit from these elements that provide comfort and allow them to cope.

Involve Children in Activities

Being involved means taking actions related to the loss or death. Most adults and children feel a sense of helplessness when a loss or death occurs. This is natural, since in most circumstances we can't do anything to replace the loss or keep our loved one from dying. Such a loss of control and hope is often associated with depression. To some degree, taking action can help individuals keep control and maintain hope in their lives.

When children move and change schools, they need to take action. Making new friends and learning new rules gives them a positive focus during a difficult time, and when they succeed, their self-esteem is increased.

Similarly, when children know someone who has died, they need to be involved in the related activities. Adults can provide positive role models for children at this time by including them in many of the activities. Children can help cook, deliver food, make cards, choose flowers, make a memorial notebook and even help choose a gravestone. Being involved provides a focus. Helping others makes children feel good about themselves.

Once again, think about a child's level of understanding before you decide what activities to offer. Do not force children to participate in these activities, but always offer them the *opportunity* to participate.

Many children will want to. They like to imitate their parents and teachers; they want to feel a part of things.

Tell children what you plan to do, why you do it, and possibly how it makes you feel. Then let children know how they can help if they want to. Most children will be either curious or flattered enough to take action. It's also OK if they're not interested. When they are ready, they will accept your offer.

What about the funeral itself? Should children be involved in the funeral too? It depends. Consider questions such as these: What type of service will it be? Will adults be available to support children during the service? If the funeral is to be a long, formal, religious ceremony, it might not be realistic to expect a young child to sit through it. If the ceremony involves participation by the guests and has the feel of a celebration, this might be a problem for a child who is quiet or who is very angry and traumatized by the death. But other children might feel comfortable in the same situation.

Use your knowledge of the child and your intuition to decide whether the specific circumstances are ones that the child can handle. Before you encourage children to attend the funeral, make sure that an adult will be available to provide support during the service. Funerals can arouse unexpected feelings in both adults and children. An adult should be standing by in case a child needs help.

When the conditions and support are appropriate and a child does attend funeral services, it can be a powerful teaching tool. Children will have the opportunity to watch how adults comfort each other, comfort themselves and grieve. Children can see and learn a variety of responses and experience their own feelings in the situation. None of the planned learning activities you might provide for children can be as influential as these real experiences. Planned activities, however, still have an important role in children's development. They help prepare and/or "debrief" children for when real death occurs.

Use Memories for Comfort

Adults may put memories on hold and bring them out when they can cope with them. Children need their memories kept close at hand. Memories of the love and comfort they received from the person who died are especially helpful. Often by remembering the love and comfort, children are able to still feel loved and comforted. It's reassuring to know that these feelings don't disappear when loved ones die.

Even hurtful memories can be important to children. Even if their grief for the deceased includes unpleasant feelings, the memories are still important. Children are much more frightened by a lack of memories.

If no one talks about Uncle Joe, possibly because he was an unpleasant person to be around, children might conclude that if they themselves are not "good," no one will remember them. They may not be able to verbalize such a feeling; it may be only an uncomfortable feeling somewhere in the subconscious. But the underlying attitude they will have learned is that life and death are insignificant.

On the other hand, acknowledging the memories acknowledges the importance of the losses. Learning to use memories for comfort is a step toward successfully handling feelings of loss. Just as mastery of math concepts builds self-esteem, mastery of difficult feelings can build self-esteem.

Keeping memories alive also helps children acknowledge that the dead person was an important part of their lives, and allows them to let go of the person gradually. Memories can fill some of the empty spaces left when someone dies. As time goes by, memories may be needed less frequently, but remembering will always be an important way of coping with loss and death.

Chapter 4

Responding to Children's Questions

This chapter offers guidelines for discussing death with children and provides suggestions for answering the specific questions they might ask. You will also find a section to help you replace potentially harmful indirect or symbolic language with direct language.

Guidelines for Discussing Death with Children

When talking to younger children, use concrete terms and short answers. You will often find yourself giving information in response to facial expressions or behavior instead of direct questions. Young children may be unable to put their questions or feelings in words; look to their actions for clues. And often your tone of voice and the physical comfort you can offer will be more important than the exact words you use.

For older children, give answers that leave room for their concepts to grow. It's OK to use some words they might not know, if you're in a situation where they can ask questions to clarify. Try to find out what brought the question to the child's mind. The reason for asking can help you decide how much detail to give.

Make sure you know what children are really asking. Ask questions to clarify what you have heard. As always, answer in an open atmosphere with the familiar expressions of comfort you usually use—touches, hugs, smiles, a loving tone of voice. It may sometimes seem as if the words you're saying and the things you're describing don't go along with a calm, reassuring tone. But children need to know that what you're saying or describing is *not* too awful to talk about.

Balance emotions with matter-of-factness. Even though death is a difficult topic, we can still talk about it and try to understand and feel better together. Take some time for yourself. If necessary, choose another time for your discussion with the children—when you're more able to think about their needs. This doesn't mean that you should show no emotion at all. But for children to be able to hear the whole message, a degree of control is needed. If you're too emotional, they can't understand the words. On the other hand, if you show no emotion, the words may seem too harsh or be confusing.

When children ask a question about feelings, focus on emotional answers and support. When their questions are factual, focus on informative answers. Even if what they ask surprises you, try to accept it as important and give the thoughtful answers children's questions deserve.

Be honest, truthful and loving. Regardless of the type of question or the developmental stage of the child, your answers should be honest, truthful and loving. After listening carefully to a child's questions or comments, decide whether you should give explanations or comfort or ask more questions to be sure you understand the question. Try not to worry about having the right answers; if you speak honestly and from your heart, your answer will be meaningful. Sincerity can make up for any awkwardness, and it leaves the door open for further questions as needed.

The only questions or comments you should not be accepting of are those showing that the child feels responsible for the death. When this occurs, you must be very direct and forceful—making sure the child understands that he or she is not to blame. Repeat the message as often as necessary until you're sure it is understood, and that the real cause (if known) is accepted by the child.

Although children need to learn both facts and emotional coping skills related to death, they may be able to concentrate on only one aspect at a time. Over time you'll be able to touch on all the important elements of teaching children about death. Remember, all children are aware of death at some level. They may be too young to put their questions into words, or they may be old enough but too quiet or shy. But they are aware of and thinking about the death-related experiences in their lives. Your job is to interpret their questions and behavior and provide or look for opportunities to give the information and support they need at each step toward understanding death as a natural part of life.

Use direct, meaningful language. The following table gives suggestions for using direct language in place of the indirect or symbolic. This eliminates a lot of fear and confusion for children; it allows them to develop a positive, realistic understanding of death.

Using Direct, Meaningful Language		
Instead of...	**Say...**	**Because...**
asleep	died	child may fear sleep
in heaven	died and/or buried	beliefs have to be explained separately
lost	died	child may continue to look for missing person, or wonder why adults aren't still looking, creates fear of "Wouldn't they look for me if I was lost?"
old	specific cause like heart attack	age twenty seems old to a child
on journey	died	child may fear trips
passed away	died	vagueness encourages harmful imagination to fill in gaps
sick	heart stopped beating; lungs wouldn't work; too sick for doctors to make well	child has difficulty distinguishing between a simple cold and life-threatening illness

Examples of Questions and Responses

Following are some examples of typical questions asked by children at different developmental stages. The actual questions children ask will depend not only on their stage of understanding but on the level of their emotional involvement and the circumstances surrounding the specific death-related event. Remember, the age ranges are not rigid. They are just reference points to indicate the steps in how children learn about death. The progression is similar no matter what age range is presented.

In each set of examples, try your hand at answering the questions before reading the suggested answers. Remember also that the answers given are only examples of the responses that would be appropriate for the child's level of understanding. They are not meant to be memorized. Look at the style of language and the content of the answers. Use these samples as a basis for your ideas, ideas put into your own words— including your own examples, feelings and beliefs where needed.

Typical Questions from Children Under Age Three

Where is Grandpa, Mommy?

He's dead, honey. He's in heaven.

When is Grandpa coming back?

He's dead, honey; he won't ever come back. We won't ever see him again. But we'll always miss him.

Why are you crying, Mommy?

Because Uncle Joe died today and it makes me very sad to think that I'll never see him again or hear him laugh.

Daddy, why won't Mommy play with me today?

Mommy is too sad to play today because her uncle died. She'll play with you another day. Today, I'll play with you. Let's get out the blocks.

Typical Questions from Children Ages Three Through Five

Why is Uncle Don so upset?

Because Grandma is dead and he won't ever see her again.

Should I be crying too?

Only if you feel like it. Some people do and some don't. It's OK either way.

Where is Grandma?

She's dead. Her body is buried and her spirit is in heaven.

When is Grandma coming home?

She won't ever come home. She's dead and her body is buried in that cemetery over by the park.

Why did Grandma go away now? We haven't had my birthday party yet.

She didn't go away, she died. Her heart was too weak to keep beating. When your heart stops beating your body doesn't work any more and you die. I know Grandma would be sorry to miss your birthday party. We'll all miss Grandma, too.

What happened to Blackie?

Blackie was in the street and a car ran over him. He's dead now.

Do rocks die when cars run over them?

No, rocks are never living so they can't die. Rocks don't breathe and move around like you and I do—like Blackie used to. But now Blackie is dead and he won't ever breathe or move around anymore.

You mean Blackie isn't going to get up and follow us home now?

No, we'll have to carry him home and have a funeral for him.

What's a funeral?

A funeral is a way people say goodbye to someone who dies. It's also a way to say how much we loved the one who died. We'll have a funeral for Blackie. I'll show you.

_____

Why didn't Grandpa keep the lucky rabbit's foot he gave me? Then he wouldn't have to die.

Luck doesn't have anything to do with dying. Grandpa died because his whole body was so sick, for such a long time, and the doctors couldn't make him well anymore.

_____

Aunt Martha lied to me. She promised we'd bake cookies today after school, but now she's dead.

She didn't lie to you. She didn't know she was going to die. But today when she was coming home from the grocery store her car was hit by a big truck and the accident killed her.

Was she buying the chocolate chips at the grocery store?

I don't know. Why?

If she didn't have to get chocolate chips for our cookie baking, she wouldn't be dead.

Aunt Martha's death has nothing to do with you! She died because of a terrible accident. She bought chocolate chips for you lots of days and never had an accident before. You didn't have anything to do with the accident. Do you understand?

Yes. Now who will bake cookies with me?

I will. Today, let's bake some cookies and take them to Uncle Phil and Cousin Lynn. They must be very sad, and our cookies will remind them that we love them.

Responding to Children's Questions _____ 71

Are you sick, Daddy?

I just have a little sore throat.

Are you going to die, Daddy?

I don't expect to die until I'm a very old man. This sore throat will certainly not kill me. The doctor gave me some medicine and I'm feeling better already.

When Grandpa got sick, he took medicine and he died anyway.

I know, but Grandpa was much sicker than I am. His heart was too sick to keep beating and his lungs were too sick to keep breathing. You can live with a sore throat. You can't live without breathing lungs and a beating heart.

Why does Grandma's old room make me feel so sad?

I don't know—let's talk about it. What do you think of when you're in there?

I remember playing games and reading stories together.

Was that fun for you?

Yes.

Does anyone else play and read like Grandma did?

No.

Sounds like you're missing that special kind of fun that you had only with Grandma.

Yeah! I really miss Grandma—I wish she'd come back.

I know what you mean. I really miss her too. I miss her so much that it still makes me cry sometimes. I wish she could come back, but she can't. But it does make me feel better to remember our fun together. When I was a little girl, I used to love the way Grandma read *The Pokey Little Puppy*. What was your favorite story?

Typical Questions from Children Ages Six Through Eight

How did Patty's mother die?

She had cancer. The cancer cells started taking over the healthy cells of her body until her body just couldn't keep working anymore.

Why didn't the doctors just zap the cancer cells?

They tried several types of treatment but it wasn't enough. Sometimes it works. This time it didn't.

What will happen to her body now?

Her body will be taken to a funeral home. The people there will put her in a casket for the funeral and burial.

Will we go to the funeral?

I will be going to the funeral. I will be going to the visitation also. You may go with me to the funeral or the visitation if you want to. Or you can stay at John's house while I go.

What do you do at a visitation?

I will visit with Patty and her family at the funeral home. Her mother's dead body will be there in a casket. I'll go to the casket and look at Kathy for a while—it's sort of like saying goodbye to her even though she can't hear us talking to her or see us standing there. Then I'll tell Patty and her father that I am sad too and that I will be glad to help out if they need anything. There will be other people there doing similar things to show the family that they care.

Why is everyone dressed up? (at the funeral)

It's one of the ways we show our respect for the feelings of the family.

Why is everyone so quiet? (at the funeral home)

Some people are showing their respect, some are just thinking their own thoughts.

Why did they cut her legs off? (looking at half-open casket)

They didn't cut her legs off. This is just a traditional way of showing the body in the casket. The legs are underneath the closed half. (If the child is close family, you may ask the funeral director to open the other half to show the child that the legs are still there.)

Why can't we see inside the casket? (looking at closed casket)

The family decides whether the casket should be open or closed. When they decide to have it closed it's because they think it's more respectful, or they just want to remember the dead person as they looked when they were alive instead of lying in the casket.

What is cremation?

When someone dies, some people choose to have the body put in a casket and buried in a cemetery. Others choose to have the body cremated. That means the body is burned into ashes. But remember, it doesn't hurt—the person is dead and doesn't have feelings anymore. Sometimes the ashes are kept in the family's home and sometimes they are buried or kept in a mausoleum or crypt.

Why do we put flowers on Grandma's grave if she can't see them anyway?

Putting flowers on Grandma's grave helps us remember how much we loved her and how much we miss her. It reminds us that she is still an important part of our lives even if she isn't with us anymore.

I haven't felt happy since Daddy died. When will I feel happy again?

I don't know when, but you will, someday. Remember, even though we're unhappy about Daddy dying, I know Daddy would want you to get back to being the happy kid you used to be. You'll still have sad times when you miss Daddy. But you'll also have memories of Daddy that will make you happy. And you'll learn to do new things and make new friends that will make you happy too.

I'm never going to speak to Aunt Doris again! If she had taken Grandpa to the hospital last night he wouldn't have died. It's all her fault!

I know you're angry about Grandpa dying. But there are two important things you need to know about what happened last night. First, Grandpa was going to die no matter what we did. His lungs were getting weaker and weaker until they finally quit working altogether. Also, Grandpa told Aunt Doris not to take him to the hospital. He didn't want a machine to breathe for him and have to live the rest of his life in a hospital bed.

You mean Grandpa wanted to die? I don't believe Grandpa would ever want to give up and die.

No, he didn't want to die. But he knew that his body wasn't capable of taking care of itself anymore. It was his time to die and he accepted that. He didn't give up; he just understood.

Typical Questions from Children Age Nine and Over

Will Grandpa see Grandma now that he's in heaven?

I don't know for sure, but I think that's what it's like. That's what I believe.

Why is Joe laughing? Doesn't he care that Grandpa died?

Yes, he cares. People respond in different ways. He might be laughing because he's nervous. Or he might be laughing because someone told a funny story about Grandpa and he knows Grandpa would want him to carry on with a happy life. People have a lot of different emotions when they're mourning. There aren't any wrong ones. Everyone just handles their grief the best way they can. Do you want to tell me how you're feeling?

How can I go ahead with my plans for my go-cart now that Uncle Phil is dead?

I know Uncle Phil was a big part of your plans for the go-cart rally. But he wouldn't want you to quit now. He'd want you to find another partner and finish what the two of you had planned. That way it will always be something you can remember about Uncle Phil because he got you started. What do you think?

Why doesn't anyone ever talk about Uncle Phil anymore?

Talking about Uncle Phil makes some people very sad all over again, so they avoid it. Your father and I do talk about Uncle Phil because we have a lot of happy memories that we want to remember. It makes us feel good to remember the wonderful friend and brother we used to have. I guess we've been doing our remembering when you're not around. Would you like us to share that with you?

Why does Aunt Martha still talk about Uncle Phil all the time?

Maybe talking about Uncle Phil makes her feel like part of him is still here. It's hard for her to be without him. Talking about him and remembering the good times they had together makes her feel happy. She doesn't really talk about him *all* the time. As time goes by she'll talk about him less, but right now it's really helping her to talk about him.

You mean, someday she'll forget about him and get married to someone else?

No, she'll never forget him or the love they shared. One way to keep the memories is to talk about them. Over time she'll need to talk about him less, but she'll never forget completely. She may get married to someone else someday, but she'll still remember Uncle Phil.

What can I do to help Cousin Lynn feel better?

Just keep being the good friend you've always been and make sure she knows we still care about her. For a while it might be good to spend more time with her than usual. Can you think of anything special we might do to make her feel better?

Well, I know Uncle Phil used to take her for ice cream and to the park on Saturdays. Maybe we could take her now.

That's a good idea. She might not want to go with someone else. But it's a good idea to ask her about it.

Are You Sad Too?

Chapter 5

Using Planned Learning Activities

Both teachers and parents can create opportunities to teach children about death. This chapter offers suggestions for preparing and using planned learning activities. Teachers will be more likely to use these planned programs, but parents might also use the information to help them start conversations with their children. First you'll find a discussion of appropriate activities, then ways to prepare for the activities you choose. Next, there are key concepts to emphasize in the lessons learned in each activity. The final sections are brief descriptions of activities grouped by topic area—facts, feelings, beliefs and coping skills.

The activities are arranged based on their primary focus. However, there is overlap among the topics. Use the suggested activities as a source of ideas. They will help you discover the variety of ways you can present loss and death in learning activities for children.

Choosing Appropriate Activities

Because of your special understanding of the children you work with, you're the best person to judge which activities to use, and when. The general suggestions below will help you make decisions and prepare for your learning activities.

As you already know, for the lesson to be effective, children must be able to understand the lesson you have planned. Think about how many steps your children have already taken and what step they can take next. Remember when you refer to the stages described in Chapter 2 that age is not necessarily the best indicator; it's just a reference point. The sequence of steps taken is what you should consider when evaluating children's readiness for a lesson.

Sequence of activities is as important for you as it is for the children. To be comfortable with the topic so that you can create the open atmosphere children need to be able to explore freely, start with the less emotional activities about facts and beliefs. As you get a feel for the children's ability to understand and cope with the topic, you'll become aware of your own ability to manage sensitive issues. As you all become more comfortable, you can progress to more abstract and emotional activities about feelings and coping skills.

In addition to sequence and developmental level of the activity, you'll be deciding on appropriate topic areas. Do children need to develop a base of facts or do they need to learn to express feelings? Should you teach about beliefs or coping skills?

These questions are easier to answer when children bring up the subject of loss and death themselves. If they are expressing feelings, you respond with feeling-oriented activities. If they are asking concrete questions, you respond with fact-oriented activities.

When you're planning a sequence of activities unrelated to a specific event, it's a little more complicated. The decision depends on the children involved. Some children are comfortable with and experienced in expressing feelings. Others may need concrete facts to begin with before they will be able to explore the feelings that the facts arouse. A general guideline would be to begin with facts and beliefs, follow up with feelings, then move to coping skills.

Preparing Yourself

Once you've decided on the developmental level and the topic area, prepare the appropriate materials and environment for the activity. You might provide some starter ideas for children in some activities; in other activities you may decide to leave the activity open-ended to let the children's involvement and interests determine the direction of discussion. As with other sensitive topics, check school district policy about guidelines for informing parents before implementing any of the activities.

Some activities can be used in more than one way—focused on either children's feelings or children's knowledge about death-related concepts. But choose one focus or the other. And remember to let the children explore one step at a time. Most important, remember that the activities presented are just suggestions; adapt them to meet your own needs and style. You are best qualified to make decisions about topics and techniques; you are the one who knows what you can handle, what your children can handle, and how much time you have available.

Refer to Chapter 7 for suggestions on selecting and using children's stories to teach about loss and death. Some of the same tips apply when evaluating and selecting a video. And do more than preview your materials. Make sure you know the video or book content, dialogue and images very well.

When you're previewing, pay attention to the particular details you want to focus on, but also be aware of any feelings that might be aroused in the children or in yourself. Identify any information that might present a biased view. The material might still be useful provided you're aware of the slant and can compensate for it.

Since children will surprise you with their responses, consider as many possible responses as you can. If you feel you need more background information to tackle an activity, use the Suggested Readings and the References at the back of the book to help you with your research.

Loss and death learning activities at school may also arouse emotions in parents and caregivers. If this is not recommended by your district guidelines, consider sending a note home letting adults know about the activities you have planned at school. This is more than just a courtesy to help parents and caregivers prepare for the questions children bring home. If the parents are prepared, they may be more open; the child then has the double benefit of an open atmosphere at school and at home.

After the activities, consider sending home a note sharing children's responses with the parents. This would be a good topic for a newsletter if your school has one.

Getting Started

Before beginning an activity, introduce the topic and the activity to the children. Let them know what will take place during the activity—for example: "We'll read a story, then we'll do some pretending and some artwork to help us think about our feelings." When the topic is feelings or beliefs, consider using some of the following kinds of statements when introducing the activity:

- This activity deals with feelings about losses and deaths in your life.

- There are no right or wrong answers. All your feelings [or beliefs] are OK.

- Don't worry about agreeing with someone else's answers. Just be honest with yourself about your feelings [or beliefs].

- The important part of the activity is for you to find out how you feel and what you believe about losses and deaths in your life.

If the story is very sad or if a child in your group has had a similar experience, some children may become upset and even cry. If you think this is possible, you will want to discuss it before you begin the activity. Maybe younger children can get a comforting stuffed toy or blanket to hold during a story. Remind the children that it's OK to feel sad, to cry, or even to not feel sad. All their feelings are OK, and teachers or parents will be glad to give hugs as needed. You may have your own special way of dealing with this issue; just be sure the children feel as safe and comfortable as possible.

Even when activities are discussed, have children give their written work or art to you. When you review it you can see any reactions that weren't brought up in discussion. If there are products from the activity, such as essays or pictures, display them at home or school. Consider including a description of the activity and the children's responses in a newsletter to parents (if you are a teacher) or a note to a teacher (if you are a parent). When parents and teachers are communicating and working together, the environment for the child's exploration is expanded.

Emphasizing the Lessons Learned

Your discussion may bring out additional ideas. Be sure to include them when summarizing or emphasizing the lessons learned. As you end the activity, consider comments to the children like the following. Change the ideas into your own words as needed.

- Thank you for sharing your feelings [thoughts].

- Talking about loss and death can be hard sometimes. Maybe this activity [game, story] will make it easier for you to talk about these things on another day.

- We talked about many different feelings [facts, beliefs].

- All of your feelings [thoughts] are important.

- Your feelings and beliefs make you unique or special.

- It's important for you to take time to think about how you feel [what you think].

- Maybe you changed your ideas as you listened to others describe what they thought. Or maybe you realized how strongly you feel or believe in something because you weren't willing to change your views.

- It's important to understand your own feelings [thoughts] and the feelings [thoughts] of others. You don't have to agree with others, but understanding what they think can be interesting and helpful.

- Maybe you've thought of some questions you want to ask other adults. Who do you want to ask?

- If you think of some new questions or feelings tomorrow, or another day, we can talk about this some more. All you have to do is ask.

- Feelings are an important part of us.

- You did a nice job of sharing your feelings and listening to others' feelings.

- It's important to share our feelings with others. Sometimes it can make us feel less sad or lonely. Sometimes it can help us remember a special happiness.

- It's important to respect [care about] the feelings of others.

- Sometimes we think that only "good" feelings are OK. But that's not true. All our feelings are an important part of us. Sometimes the feelings we think are "bad" turn out not to be so bad when we say them out loud.

- Things we do can be "bad" if they hurt another person. But our feelings aren't "bad." For example, if we're really mad at someone, it's OK to be really mad. But it's not OK to hit the person.

Try not to leave the children with unanswered questions or unclarified concepts. (Refer to Teaching Facts in Chapter 3 for advice on finding clues to the child's understanding.) Remember that children may try to fill in the gaps by using their imaginations. Make sure you ask questions to check their understanding, and give them opportunities to ask questions to clarify for themselves. In addition to being clear, it's a good idea to end an activity by reinforcing the important messages it teaches.

Activities About Facts

—WORD GAMES—

This activity is designed to help clarify concepts for children in the six-through-eight and nine-and-over stages. It can help them develop the vocabulary needed to ask questions and learn facts related to loss and death. When preparing for this activity, familiarize yourself with as many terms and definitions as you can.

Ask children to help you make a list of words they hear when people are talking about loss and death. Write down the words as the children say them. Follow up by discussing all the words until an accurate definition is clearly formed for each. You may want to divide the children into small groups or pairs to come up with definitions of words before you discuss the definitions as a whole group. A crossword puzzle or word search puzzle makes a good closing or review.

Consider these possible variations: For older children you could list various beliefs of life after death or beliefs regarding funeral rituals. Follow-up would include the same type of clarifying and defining. Remember: no judgment, just description. This could also be a follow-up activity for a reading assignment, defining key terms in the assignment.

When closing the activity, stress the importance of learning to use the words correctly so that people can ask questions and better understand loss- and death-related concepts.

—FUNERAL HOME VISIT—

This activity is designed for children in the six-through-eight and nine-and-over stages who have had some experience or background education in the area of death. It is not an activity for unexperienced teachers or students, but it is an excellent activity as an advanced part of a death education curriculum. A visit to a funeral home will help children learn the physical facts about what a funeral home looks like and what happens there. It also may increase their comfort level and decrease the anxiety many people feel at the thought of going to a funeral home.

If you're a teacher taking a group of students, you'll need to follow your school district guidelines for field trips. In addition to getting consent for children to travel, it's important to let parents know the purpose of the trip. Let parents know what the children will be seeing and how they will be cared for during the visit.

Parents may take a child to a funeral home to get help with answers if the child has repeated questions. Or if there is a death in the family, a visit prior to the funeral may help a child be prepared for the funeral or visitation.

The way you prepare a child for this type of visit will have a great impact on how successful the visit is. First visit the funeral home by yourself. Talk to the person who will be talking to the children. Find out whether the funeral home has any children's programs or if any of the staff have experience or training with children. If they do, well and good. If they don't, you may have to prepare the funeral director for how to talk to children in general. Giving the director a sampling of the kinds of questions your children may ask is a good approach. If you're uncomfortable with the way the staff handles any questions, visit other funeral homes until you find one that you would consider a positive experience for the children.

Before the tour, be sure to establish with the director what the tour will and won't include. For example, you may want to include the embalming room for children in the nine-and-over stage, but not those in the six-through-eight stage. The area where new coffins are stored is another place you may or may not want to visit. Just being in the funeral home may be enough for a first visit.

As children get older, or more experienced, or have more questions, they will want to see more parts of the facility. Talk to older children to see what they're interested in. Make sure they know they have a choice about how much they see. For the younger children, clearly explain what it will be like on the tour. Tell who will talk to them and what room or rooms they will see. Tell them what type of furnishings they'll see. Tell them what rooms they won't see. Especially assure them that they *won't* see a dead body. Ask the children to write down questions they would like to ask. This list will help prepare you and the funeral home guide.

Be sure you have plenty of adult chaperones available for this type of field trip. You may have to divide the group at some time. For example, while some children may want to see the coffins, others won't. The children should not be forced. You'll need extra adults to supervise the children who don't want to see everything the funeral director offers.

Prepare the children for contingencies. You may have scheduled your visit ahead of time but if the funeral home has a funeral to conduct, your visit may be canceled. Or some children may feel prepared and then have different feelings when they are actually there. Talk ahead of time about what do you do if...you change your mind about going with one group...you feel sad...you feel like laughing, etc. Encourage children to speak up and then reassure them: Since there will be no mourners at the funeral home at the time of our visit, you won't risk offending anyone if you laugh. If you feel sad, for whatever reason, it's OK. If you change your mind, say so and you can return to the group in the waiting area.

Once you're in the funeral home, with plenty of supportive adults, and well-prepared children, let the funeral home guide take over. He or she will tell about the jobs and the facility, just like a field trip to another place of business. Your job is to watch the children to see that they're understanding the information and handling the situation. You may need to clarify a child's question, or clarify the staff person's response. If the children are too shy to ask their questions, you might want to ask the questions they gave you in class. Help the guide address the children's interests and keep the discussion at their level of understanding.

Follow-up after the visit is critical. Be sure to give children plenty of time to ask more questions. If you don't know the answers, write down the questions and ask the funeral director or the guide. Although this discussion is focused on learning the facts, you should let the children express whatever ideas or feelings were aroused by the visit. You may ask them to write about their visit or draw something to get more clues as to whether they fully understood or if they have some misconceptions.

In addition to clarifying the facts about what happens in a funeral home, your discussion should reinforce the concept that death is a natural part of life, and that this is what happens, physically, when someone dies.

—CEMETERY VISIT—

Children in the six-through-eight or nine-and-over stages can benefit from this activity. The goal is to teach children about the different ways people bury their loved ones. Teachers may schedule a formal field trip, following school district guidelines for such trips. Parents may make an informal visit to a cemetery, possibly even a visit to a cemetery where relatives are buried.

To prepare for the trip, visit the cemetery yourself first. Take a walk around the grounds and decide on specific things to point out to the children. To prepare the children, tell them where you're going and what they'll be seeing. Give the children time to talk—telling what they know about cemeteries and asking questions. Try to find out whether anyone is afraid of the trip, or if anyone knows someone buried in the cemetery you'll be visiting.

Spring is a good time for this outdoor field trip because of weather and because cemeteries are often naturally pretty during this season. When things are bright and growing, it becomes less somber, allowing children to think about the physical details you want to teach.

If you can provide plenty of adult chaperones, you will have the option of dividing the group into smaller groups for exploring. If you do this, make a list of the details you want the other adults to point out to children in each group.

Check with the groundskeeper or cemetery manager to schedule your visit. If a funeral is scheduled, they will inform you. Respect the grieving family, and change your visit to a different time of day or a different day. Seeing an open grave may be interesting for older children, but it should be done before the graveside service begins.

Some suggestions for details to look for and point out to children include different sizes of grave markers or monuments, unusually shaped monuments, individual mausoleums, a community mausoleum, urns of ashes, varying epitaphs, decorations, flat markers, religious symbols or words used. Let children walk around and see the differences. You might ask them to find an example of some of the items listed above. Or ask them to find the marker or epitaph that they like best. After you've explored, sit for a while and talk. Let the children direct the discussion. Write down any questions you don't know the answer to and get the answers for the children later.

Reinforce the lesson by closing with a description of the different types of burials, markers and epitaphs. Remind the children that these are personal and religious decisions which people have made. The variety represents the great variety of individuals who are buried in the cemetery. The type of burial is an honor to the individual who is buried.

—What Do You See on the News?—

The main purpose of this activity is to show children that death is a part of our lives, and thus it's important to learn about what happens when people die. If you want to extend the activity, you can go into more detail about news articles focusing on facts. The activity is designed for the six-through-eight and nine-and-over stages.

Tell children to look through a newspaper or listen to or watch the evening news. Ask them to look for stories that have a loss or a death in them and stories that use death-related words when they're not really referring to death. When you make this assignment, take some time to talk about some of the examples they might find. Have older children make a list of the stories and words they found. Ask younger children to remember two stories to tell about in class.

On the following day have children present their stories and words to the class. Make a list of them on newsprint or the board. Referring to your completed list, make the point that loss and death are a part of our daily lives. Note that we would find just as many stories on any day of the week. Although we are fortunate not to have to deal with the personal sadness on a daily basis, we need to know that loss and death are a real part of life.

If you want to extend the lesson, you have some options. You might start by stating that because death is part of our lives we need to know what happens when a person dies. This can lead you into a study unit on beliefs or funeral rituals. Another extension would be to discuss the cause of the losses and deaths in the news. You could identify which causes are preventable and which are not. Or you could focus on the various actions people take when a loss or death occurs.

Regardless of your approach, the overall theme is that while loss and death are extremely emotional and often quite sad, they are still part of our lives. We need to learn how to get and give comfort and understand the related events. In this way we learn that life goes on after loss and death.

Activities About Beliefs

—COMPARING BELIEFS AND RITUALS—

This activity is designed to introduce children to the concept that people have different death-related beliefs and rituals. It is best suited to give children in the three-through-five and the six-through-eight stages practice in expressing their own beliefs and identifying beliefs and rituals that are different from their own. When preparing for this activity, you may want to read about the beliefs and practices of other cultures.

Read two stories to children that include different cultural or religious beliefs and practices related to death. (See Chapter 7 and the Suggested Readings for ideas.) Ask the children to help you make a list of the beliefs and practices described in each story. Then discuss and compare the beliefs and practices in the two stories. To continue the activity, ask the children if they know of additional practices that weren't included in the stories.

When you close the activity remember to stress the variety of practices and the comfort provided by beliefs and practices.

—INTERVIEW YOUR FAMILY—

This activity will help children see how their families' backgrounds determine their beliefs. It is most appropriate for the six-through-eight and nine-and-over stages. You may want to prepare a letter to parents explaining the assignment. Be sure parents know that the beliefs are not going to be evaluated, just discussed. Some children may need to find a neighbor or adult friend to interview if their parents are unavailable.

Tell the children you want to find out about all the different beliefs people have related to death. Ask the children to help you come up with a list of questions that you'd all like to know the answers to. Have the children take the list of questions home and interview an adult. When the interviews are completed, ask the children to share their results with the class. Stress the variety of beliefs and practices and how our culture and/or religion help us decide what's right for us.

You could adapt the activity by having the children interview their families regarding experiences, feelings or any other concept related to loss or death.

As you end the activity, suggest that the children reflect on their own beliefs. Have them write a descriptive paragraph or answer some of the following questions in discussion or writing: Were any of your parents' answers new to you? Did you hear any different views in class that might make you change your own beliefs? How did you feel about beliefs that were different from yours or those of your parents? What do you believe at this moment?

—Death in Different Cultures—

This activity challenges children in the nine-and-over stage to explore the death-related beliefs of different cultures. Begin with your regular social studies book. Whether you're studying Native Americans or ancient or world cultures, take time to look at the way those cultures view(ed) death. If your current text doesn't include references to death, look through some older social studies texts (an early 1970s edition would be a likely source).

Ask children to tell you what they know about how Americans deal with death. What happens to the body? What is a funeral like? How is burial done? What do people do when they grieve? Do they know how Native Americans or ancient Egyptians dealt with death? Since they're not likely to know much about this, make a research assignment. To create interest in this activity, describe a Viking funeral pyre set out to sea—children often find this exciting.

Divide the topic by culture (Native Americans, Romans, etc.) or by part of the ritual (preparation of the body, burial, processions, eulogy, etc.). Let children work in groups on different parts of this assignment. In addition to text books, you will find this type of information in some of the nonfiction children's books about death and dying. If you think your children will have trouble finding material, consider bringing items into class for them (old social studies texts, nonfiction children's books, biographies, past and present newspapers, etc.).

You can extend the idea to compare information in obituaries today and those printed at the turn of the century. Or use biographies to find out about the funerals of famous people like U.S. presidents or Roman leaders or Chinese emperors. Then make comparisons.

When the research is done, have children present their material to the class orally. Make a chart on the board comparing the different cultures. Talk about why certain cultures may believe or do what they do. Is it related to religious beliefs? Is it because of limited knowledge? Is it because of fear? What else do you know about the culture that might affect beliefs and rituals related to death?

In closing, reinforce the idea that differences in the way people deal with death are the result of their broader culture. These traditions and rituals aren't good or bad, they're just different and are often quite interesting.

Activities About Feelings

—FINISH THE SENTENCE—

This activity is appropriate for the six-through-eight and nine-and-over stages because of the need for reading skills. You could do the activity orally with small groups in the three-through-five stage also. Depending on the focus you choose, this activity is designed to help you understand what the children feel or know. It also gives children the chance to practice expressing themselves, think about other's views and/or learn some new facts.

After you decide whether you want to focus on feelings or knowledge, develop a list of open-ended questions. Prepare a written handout of your questions. Before you present the activity to the class, try filling in the sentences yourself—write your own answers as well as some possible children's responses.

Give the children a list of incomplete sentences with blank spaces at the end. For example: When I watch a television show about a divorce I feel _____. Ask the children to fill in the blanks in each sentence by describing their feelings. Follow up their written work with a discussion, listing the various responses on the board or a newsprint pad. Divide the children into pairs or small groups to discuss their answers before you discuss them with the whole group.

Another variation would be to substitute factual sentences for feeling sentences. For example: When a dead body is cremated it is _____. The number of open-ended statements you use will depend on time available for the activity and the abilities of the children. Select statements that are either most appropriate for your children's stage and interest, or that focus on your teaching goal.

As you end the activity, remember to provide positive reinforcement for the children's participation. Note the variety of responses and the wealth of knowledge and/or compassion they have about the subject. As long as none of the feelings mentioned include responsibility for a death, be sure to maintain your open atmosphere, accepting and respecting all feelings. Conclude with a clear statement about all feelings being OK and the importance of sharing them.

—Feelings in Children's Stories—

The following activities are most appropriate for the middle two stages— three through five and six through eight. They are designed to give children practice in expressing their feelings and thinking about how others might feel.

Read a children's story that includes examples of loss- or death-related situations. (Refer to Chapter 7 for lists of suggested books.) Ask the children to listen to how the different characters feel about what happens. Follow the story with a discussion of how the feelings were presented in the story. How did you know what the characters felt? Was it from pictures or expressions, words, or something else? Then ask the children to tell how they might feel if this happened to them.

If this type of activity is difficult or uncomfortable for the children, start the discussion by sharing how you would feel. Sharing your feelings can be important as long as you make sure the children know that everyone's feelings are important and accepted.

Further follow-up could include an art activity, asking children to make a picture, collage, etc., showing a feeling like one of the characters felt or showing how they would feel if they were one of the characters. Be sure to collect the artwork and display it.

When working with younger children, use paper cutouts or puppets to represent the characters in the story. Prepare a large three-column chart with feeling words at the top or varied faces like "smiley," neutral and "frowny" faces. Then, as you discuss the character's feelings, have children match the paper dolls or puppets with the feeling.

Depending on your discussion you can show how one character feels different emotions throughout the story, or how different characters feel different emotions. Either way, you stress the variety of acceptable feelings. If you want the children to think about their own feelings, they can place themselves in areas of the room already identified to represent different feelings.

Regardless of the specific approach you take, end the activity by stressing the variety of acceptable feelings. Include some of the supportive closing concepts suggested earlier.

—VIDEO ACTIVITIES—

Videos can be used for almost all stages. Just vary the length and follow-up activities. Some of the tips about using children's literature, in Chapter 7, also apply to selecting and using videos.

Select a video with examples of loss and/or death situations. Before showing the video, tell the children a little about the story. Don't give away any important secrets that might spoil the story for them, but prepare them for the possibility of sadness (if necessary).

Ask some specific questions about the feelings or actions in the story. Your questions should help children focus on the topics that you want to discuss in your follow-up activities. Follow the video by clarifying the story line; then discuss the feelings as described in the previous activity, Feelings in Children's Stories.

You can vary this activity to focus on coping skills. For younger children, ask them to make sympathy cards for the character in the video that experienced the loss or death. You may need to provide some sample sympathy cards and phrases if these are unfamiliar to the children. Be sure the children understand not to copy the samples. They need to be encouraged to express their own feelings and ideas. For older children, have them conduct a pretend funeral for the character that died in the video. Follow the descriptions of the Pretend Funeral activity at the end of this chapter.

—ALL MY FEELINGS COUNT—

The purpose of this activity is to help young children in the under-three and three-through-five stages understand the importance of feelings and the variety of acceptable feelings and to provide them with some practice at recognizing their feelings.

To prepare for this activity you'll need a group of pictures, pieces of music or smells that you think will arouse feelings in your children. You'll also need to make "feeling cards." These may have colors, words, or smiling, neutral and frowning faces. The cards could even be heart-shaped. Review each feeling card to be sure the children understand the feeling the card represents.

Begin this activity by giving each child a paper bag. Ask the children to decorate the bag by drawing a picture of themselves on the bag. Then tell them, "Today we're going to find out how music and pictures and smells can make us feel things." For each piece of music, picture, or smell that you present to the children, ask them to think for a bit, then choose a card that shows how the music or picture makes them feel. The children will keep their collection of feeling cards in their own bags.

Remind the children that each person has many different feelings at different times. A feeling doesn't stay with you all the time. If you're feeling sad, sometimes a happy song will make you happy. Or if you're angry, a funny picture will make you laugh. Sometimes our feelings affect how we act. Sometimes we're too sad to play and sometimes we're too excited to work on lessons.

As you close the activity, have children look through all their feeling cards. Can they remember some of the feelings? Consider having the children take their bag of feelings home to share with their families.

Activities About Coping Skills

—MEMORY SHOW AND TELL—

The purpose of this activity is to help children learn to express and listen to sensitive feelings. It can be adapted to use at any stage of development. In this scenario children are asked to bring up something from their past, not a current loss or death. The idea is for children to get some practice sharing feelings when the loss or death is not currently traumatic. You may need to give the children an example to help them understand the assignment.

Ask children to bring in an object or story that reminds them of something they've lost or someone who has died. Sit in a circle to make the sharing time more intimate. Tell the children that today we're going to take turns telling about our memories of something we have lost or someone who has died. Ask for volunteers to tell their stories. Encourage everyone to share their feelings, but don't force anyone to share.

Depending on the stage the children are at, you'll need to vary the content. Younger children may remember an activity or toy they miss. Children in middle stages may deal with dead pets or people. And older children may think about any of these. Another variation is to have older children share rituals they have observed.

If you're doing this assignment at school, you may want to send a note to parents about the assignment. Describe the activity and what you hope the children will learn from it. Give the parents some examples of what you have in mind for show and tell so they can help any children who may have difficulty with the assignment. Your note could also include a suggestion that the parents discuss the memories with their children before and after the school activity.

If you think children may become sad or cry, ask another trusted adult to be nearby when you do these activities. This may not be necessary, but you need to be prepared to provide the support children might need.

The emphasis of this activity is that all our feelings are important to us and that sharing feelings is helpful. However, if a child expresses the feeling of responsibility for a natural loss or death, remember to treat this feeling differently. You must tell the child that it was not his or her fault. Be alert to this possibility as the children share their stories.

As the children put away their mementos, explain that sometimes people put away their feelings too. You can put away a hurtful feeling for a while if it starts to hurt too much. Or if you feel especially sad about someone or something you're missing, you can take out a special memory you have put away and let the memory help you feel better.

—PRETEND FUNERAL—

This activity is best suited for the six-through-eight and nine-and-over stages. It could be simplified for the three-through-five stage as well. The focus is on learning about rituals by planning a pretend funeral.

Depending on the developmental stage of the children, you'll need to provide more or less structure for this activity. Older children may identify the tasks and distribute them to specific work groups by themselves. Younger children will probably have to have work groups identified and be given a list of things to do. Children in the middle stage may benefit from preestablished work groups, but let them decide on the specific tasks of each group. Start by offering broad suggestions and getting more specific until you feel the children are ready to begin action on their own.

If you're uncomfortable with this type of activity, it's not right for you. Review Chapter 1, or wait until you develop more experience or have the right group of students to handle the activity. If you think your students won't take it seriously, they're probably not ready for it either. But this activity can be appropriate and beneficial for some children, especially if there's been a series of other death education activities as preparation.

Tell the children they are going to plan a pretend funeral for a stuffed toy or a character in a story or movie. Divide the children into small groups and assign a specific part of the funeral arrangements to each group—for example, funeral home arrangements, burial, eulogy and decorations. You may need to work with each group to help them come up with a list of tasks.

You could also provide a checklist of tasks for each group. The funeral home group would plan the time of the funeral, the clothing or other preparation of body, the casket, casket lining, and visitation. The burial group plans cemetery, grave and tombstone. The eulogy group decides on the service, what should be said, and how it is to be conducted. The decorations group tasks might include flowers, music and a reception after the service.

If the children come from varied cultural and religious backgrounds, the pretend funeral may be a mixed version. It doesn't matter. Let the children come up with whatever they feel is appropriate. When closing the activity, remember to stress the variety of rituals that people follow, and how these actions and rituals often provide comfort.

Chapter 6

Responding to a Loss or a Death

We think of most deaths as occurring within the family, but the reality is that classroom pets, teachers, classmates and public figures die too—and these deaths have an effect on children. Like deaths, losses can occur in any setting as well. Therefore parents, teachers and caregivers all should be prepared to respond to losses and deaths whenever and wherever they occur.

Children actually experiencing loss and/or death need a different type of learning experience than the planned activities described in Chapter 5. Although you will still be aware of the four basic teaching areas (facts, feelings, beliefs and skills), your response to an actual loss or death will be more spontaneous and less structured. In your planned activities you had a *specific* goal for your lesson. In your responses to actual loss and death experiences, you have a *general* goal of helping the child cope with the experience positively.

You will still have to assess what the child needs. You should find out what the child is feeling and how much he or she already knows. In an actual death situation, you will need to provide immediate comfort to the child. And you will be teaching and role-modeling coping skills.

Instead of providing an artificial scenario such as a story or video, you'll help children understand specific real-life situations. Depending on your relationship to the person who died, you may also be dealing with your own reactions and feelings at the same time.

If you've already had planned activities for the child, you'll be better prepared to share a current event. If you haven't, it will be important for you to be well prepared personally to deal with loss and death concepts. If you have prepared yourself, you'll be better able to let children's needs and questions direct your responses. You'll be open to helping them understand the full range of feelings and questions aroused by the situation—allowing them to explore the experience fully, one step at a time.

This chapter deals with that "teachable moment" when a death occurs and children need help coping. You will find a discussion of the normal grieving responses people—including children—go through in response to a loss or death. You will also find some general guidelines to assist you in helping children grieve. Finally, you will find suggestions for helping children respond to death in specific situations.

The Stages of Grief

According to Elisabeth Kubler-Ross (1969), a pioneer of death education, people go through five different stages in their feelings and reactions toward a death.

Denial is the first stage. When first confronted with death we often deny the facts in an attempt to give ourselves time to adjust. We might say, "No, not me!" This is a coping mechanism we use to protect ourselves. A child might say, "I know my grandma wouldn't leave without saying goodbye. She'll be back tomorrow."

The second stage is often *anger*. Once we realize we can no longer deny the facts we become angry that this could happen to us. We might say, "Why me?" Children might say, "I hate you for saying Daddy is dead," or "I hate Daddy for dying before my big baseball game."

The third stage is *bargaining*. It is characterized by the phrase "If only..." Sometimes bargaining is done in the form of prayers, hoping for a miracle. Or it can be a promise to a doctor to cooperate in return for a week away from treatments in order to visit someone special before you become unable to travel. A child's bargain might be, "I promise to learn the multiplication tables and get one hundred percent if Mrs. Johnson can be alive today."

Next comes *depression*. When denial, anger and bargaining fail to make situations better, we may give up. Children may express their depression by not eating or not playing with friends. When depression sets in, we are acknowledging the reality and finality of death; we have stopped fighting it.

As we emerge from the sadness and loneliness of depression, we begin the fifth stage—*acceptance*. This is often a quiet, peaceful stage. It's somewhere between sadness and happiness. Although people may want to be left alone, they are not lonely as they were in depression. Acceptance is a desirable state but it can only be reached by going through the emotional stages that precede it. A child's version of acceptance might be, "I know my mother loved me. And wherever she is now I won't ever stop loving her."

Although most people go through these five stages, they go through them at different rates, just as children's understanding develops through different levels or stages. People may also go through the stages in a different sequence. Understanding these stages of grief can help you respond appropriately to the range of normal reactions to a loss or death.

When children deny loss or death, gentle reminders of the facts are more helpful than confrontation. When children are angry about a death, your considerate understanding is more helpful than reciprocating with your own anger. Bargaining can be dealt with by encouraging the child's expressions, even if the terms of the bargain can't be met. Depression requires acceptance of a child's need to be alone without abandoning the child entirely.

All these stages should be accepted as normal and healthy for children. Each stage has a purpose in helping the child reach the final acceptance required for readjusting to life without the person who died. Confronting, pressuring, returning anger and raising false hopes can make it more difficult for children to progress through these grieving stages. Listening, reassuring, accepting, understanding and respecting can make the process easier.

General Guidelines

Sincerity is critical when you are responding to a child's specific loss or death situation. When your responses are genuine, children can hear and feel your sincerity and will be more willing to trust you, learn from you and be comforted by you. Some other general guidelines include:

- Consider the child's perspective.
- Acknowledge losses directly.
- Involve children in death-related ceremonies.
- Provide choices for participation.
- Be prepared for a variety of reactions.
- Remain aware of continuing needs.
- Consider what specific relationship has been lost.
- Know when to get professional help.

Consider the Child's Perspective

Developmentally, young children have the perspective that death is not personal or final. But when they actually experience the death of a loved one or of another child, it becomes personal. In the process of their grieving, children may react with any or all of the same responses that adults do. They may deny the death, be angry about it, bargain for better circumstances, be depressed or accept it.

Identifying where children are developmentally and which stage of grieving the child is experiencing should be a guide as you help them learn to live with the changes a loss or death brings. You *must* try to see the event from their perspective if you are going to be truly helpful. When you respond based only on your adult perspective or understanding you may overreact to a child's response, applying adult meanings to the child's words or actions when that wasn't what the child meant at all. Or you may fail to react to something you see as trivial, when it is actually something quite important to the child.

These responses are not only confusing for children; they can cause children to turn their feelings inward and believe that adults just don't understand or don't really care about them. Don't hesitate to ask children for their perspective. Seeing a child's perspective is a difficult task with no concrete answers or assurances of success. But it's a task worth pursuing.

Acknowledge Losses Directly

Acknowledging loss and death is difficult for us as adults. Since children may be exposed to our hesitancy or denial, you may need to help them acknowledge the losses and death in their lives. Grieving children need to be encouraged to express their feelings and get actively involved in some of the death-related activities.

Involve Children in Death-Related Ceremonies

By asking "What can we do to show how much we cared about _____?" you're encouraging children to do something, but letting them choose *what* to do. Because children may be inexperienced at dealing with death they may need suggestions from you, for specific ways to handle the situation. By offering choices you're providing guidance without telling them exactly how to feel or what to do. Children are able to choose actions they feel will express their individual feelings in their own ways.

How far do you go with letting children be involved—as far as you can handle both emotionally and practically and as long as the children continue showing an interest. Remember, children can be involved in decision-making processes by simply being allowed to express their opinions. That doesn't mean they actually make the decisions. If you're open to letting them voice their ideas and listening to those ideas, you may be surprised at the depth of their thoughts.

When it's time to attend wakes, funerals, burials and other memorial services, keep in mind the needs of the child and the capabilities of responsible adults. The closer the relationship between the child and the person who died, the greater the need for supportive benefits that grieving rituals provide. If children will have a supportive, trusted adult available to them during a ceremony, you may let the individual children decide whether or not they will attend. If all the adults are emotionally or physically involved in the services, children should be left with people with whom they are comfortable, and not attend the memorial service.

If you aren't able to support children during services, be sure to take all opportunities to provide support after the rituals are over. As you go through pictures or the sympathy cards that have been received, you may remember parts of the service or things people said at a visitation. Share these memories with children and listen to and watch their responses. If they want to know more, you may need to describe the events completely.

If the children don't ask questions, it may mean they don't have any at the moment. They may be accepting and adapting at their own pace. In some cases, however, lack of response or questions is really a hidden response. Some children are accomplished at hiding significant feelings verbally, but their *behavior* usually gives them away. If a child spends more time in Grandpa's room or looking at Grandpa's pictures than he or she does in routine daily activities, you need to talk about it. Other children might not be used to expressing emotions and feelings at all— usually due to their family's background and culture. If they become withdrawn, you might need to initiate a discussion.

If you're not sure what children are feeling or thinking, remember your first step can always be to ask them. If they're unsure, your next step can be to read some stories to find examples. Ask if their feelings are similar to or different from the characters' feelings. Sometimes it's helpful to share your own feelings to let children see that it really is OK to say things out loud.

If you're still not getting feedback to help you understand the children's needs, check with others who spend time with them—parents ask teachers, teachers ask parents. If your attempts don't seem to be working, and you still have concerns about a child's attitude or behavior, seek professional help.

Provide Choices for Participation

When you choose to express your sympathy with a card, resist the urge to simply sign the names of children to it without talking to them. If children show little interest, signing their names is acceptable. But if they ask questions or show interest, let them get more involved. You might share your feelings about why you are sending the card, flowers or donation. Children can also be involved in making or choosing memorial gifts, or just sitting and listening as family members choose music for the funeral.

Consider other options for involving children as well. They might help select, pick or arrange flowers. They can make sympathy cards, draw pictures or write letters in memory of a loved one. Depending on the location, children can take flowers to a grave after a ceremony or ride by and visit on a bike ride. Older children might visit a grave or some other place that reminds them of their dead grandmother, in much the same way that adults do—carrying on a one-sided conversation, asking for advice or sharing their feelings with Grandma. When children sing songs that remind them of Grandpa or continue with a hobby that Grandpa started, it's a way of coping with loss and honoring the loved one.

Be Prepared for a Variety of Reactions

Children who have had a close relationship with the dead person usually will choose a way to acknowledge the death both as a memorial and for their own need to be involved in remembering and honoring the person. Children with less substantial relationships may not need to take action; the death hasn't caused as much of a loss. Children's reactions will vary. But if you have provided children with facts, a comfortable environment for their exploration, and choices for their expressions, you've done well.

Remain Aware of Continuing Needs

After the ceremonies are over, continue watching carefully as children readjust to life without the loved one. Watch for signs of understanding, lingering questions and/or the need for professional help. If children aren't "acting like themselves," if their body language or behaviors indicate that something's wrong, but they aren't telling you what's wrong or how they feel, you need to help them bring loss or death out in the open so you can explore it together.

Children's books, music and movies are good discussion starters (see Chapters 5 and 7). For example, after reading a story about a family whose grandparent died, you can ask questions and make comments to help children express their own feelings, beliefs, memories or needs. This helps move children from the general sense of loss to specific situations and/or feelings that they can agree with, disagree with, feel good about, feel sad about or any combination of these feelings. Whatever their response, they're expressing their own views or questions and taking the small steps toward understanding and acceptance.

Consider the Specific Relationship Lost

Children's perspectives and relationships to the object lost or the person who died will influence their responses. The details of the experience must be left open-ended so the children can lead you where they need to go. For example, if a pet dies, children may be concerned about the burial and possibly a memorial service. If a parent dies, children may be less concerned with rituals and more concerned about their own emotions or their own future security.

Know When to Get Professional Help

Just as you yourself respond to a variety of current experiences, you need to be aware of the variety of experiences and reactions of children. Learn how to identify whether this is a time for comfort and teaching, or a time for professional counseling. You may think that your support and teaching are enough, then find through your interactions that professional help is needed.

The best guides for knowing when to get professional help are your own intuition and your knowledge of the individual children. In general what you're looking for is *any* change in typical behavior that lasts, such as:

- not wanting to play with friends or refusing favorite activities
- not wanting to eat or refusing favorite foods
- being unable to sleep or to sleep alone
- nightmares that persist
- recurring stomachaches with no physical cause

Any or all of these behaviors can be acceptable for a limited time. They are common symptoms of grieving. The determining factors are whether the behavior is a change from a child's typical behavior before the loss or death and whether it persists, keeping the child from readjusting to life after the loss.

Specific Situations

Some examples of specific loss and death situations are presented here. Suggested responses are discussed for each situation. Remember that these are *sample* responses. Adapt the concepts and phrases to fit your situations, your personal style and your own language.

When a Special Toy Is Lost

When a young child loses an object that he or she is especially attached to—like a blanket or a teddy bear—it is an important loss in the life of that child. From an adult perspective, "It's only a stuffed toy." But from a child's perspective, "It's my sense of comfort, my confidant, my best friend, my protector while I sleep," and so on. To understand a child's perspective, think how you would feel if your best friend moved to Australia or even died? It gives you a different feeling, doesn't it?

Begin by stating the facts in a way that shows your respect for the seriousness of the situation and your acceptance of the child's feelings. Say, for example, "I'm so sorry we left Boo-Bear in the hotel. But when we called the hotel manager he said they didn't find anything. We can't fly back to Oregon to look for him." All of these comments acknowledge the child's traumatic response.

For a less severe response, simply acknowledging the loss and sadness may be enough. You'll know if you're taking the right approach by listening sensitively to the child's comments and feelings. If you're in tune with the child's perspective you'll hear the importance of his or her words.

If further actions are necessary, provide choices. You might *suggest* trying to have another stuffed toy try to do Boo-Bear's job, since Boo-Bear isn't with us anymore. If you suggest such a replacement, be sure to acknowledge that it won't be the same as Boo-Bear, but that it might make the child feel better. Some children may still reject a replacement. If so, offer other choices. Maybe a parent could lie down with the child for a few nights until the child learns that he or she will be okay without the bear. Or ask the child for suggestions about what will make him or her feel better.

As pictures or memories show up with Boo-Bear in them, remember to share both the good-feeling memories and the feelings of loss. Show your respect and acceptance. When you keep the subject open for discussion you allow children a chance to practice experiencing unpleasant or difficult feelings in a supportive environment.

When Parents Divorce or Children Must Move

When parents divorce or change jobs, children often have to move. They experience many different types of losses when they change homes. We can easily understand the loss of routines, neighborhoods and bedrooms. But what about a child who is upset about leaving new bedroom wallpaper? Is this trivial? Maybe to you as an adult, but if the child expresses this loss you need to acknowledge and respect it. Later you may find a deeper underlying reason for the concern about the wallpaper—the special time the child had while helping Dad put the paper on the walls, for example. But even if you don't understand what might be behind a child's expressed concern, respect it anyway. You can't move the bedroom with you, but you can listen and care about the child's feelings.

In addition to physical losses, when parents divorce, children may be losing the parent who played the role of confidant, or birthday cake baker, or ball player or piano teacher. To make things worse, these losses for the children come at a time when the custodial parent's strengths are reduced due to the stress of the divorce. If, on the other hand, the children's relationship with the parent who is removed was never very strong, the children's losses may center on the physical losses with only limited personal or relationship losses.

To prepare children for the various losses, explain as much as possible the details that will affect the children. Offer suggestions for ways to ease the process. If you have a custody schedule worked out, tell them when they will be with each parent. You might suggest that the child carry both parents' phone numbers so they can both be reached almost any time.

Use a calendar, even for small children, to make it more concrete and easier to understand the schedule. If children will have to move, let them go along when house- or apartment-hunting and listen to their opinions. Remember that you don't have to act on their preferences, but it is respectful to listen to them, and you might hear about something you can do to help them adjust.

Clarify which objects or furnishings will be moved and which might have to stay behind. If children will change schools, let them know what school they'll be going to as soon as you know. You can offer to go to the new school to visit and possibly meet the new teacher. You might also suggest visiting friends from the old school on weekends and/or talking to them by telephone. Try to keep surprises to a minimum. Be honest and direct about whatever details children show an interest in and those that will affect them directly.

Keep your lines of communication as open as possible, respect the children's perspective, and acknowledge the feelings and provide helpful suggestions. But even when you prepare and support as much as you can, don't expect children to accept changes instantly or easily. Just as new pets can't replace the old ones, new friends and new rooms and new stepparents can't replace the old ones.

Allow children to talk about their old neighborhood or school or to have pictures around as reminders. Maybe you miss your garden at the old house, or you miss one of your children's old friends being around. Share these feelings with your children.

Pictures and memories help children gradually let go of the old ways and adjust to the new ways at their own pace. As always, if you don't see children making progress toward adjusting to the life changes, you need professional help. But if children are adapting, however slowly, keep praising their adjustments and encouraging them to keep on taking new steps.

When a Pet Dies

One common early death experience for children is when a pet is lost or dies. As with any loss or death experience, circumstances will vary and so will the children's reactions. Although your responses can't be stated specifically for all situations, there are some general guidelines that can be helpful.

First, acknowledge the death of a pet directly. Resist the urge to replace a goldfish or hamster when the child isn't looking. Remember that it's much more frightening to think that a living creature can just disappear without notice or caring than it is to acknowledge a pet's death and related emotions. Begin by telling children the basic facts. The pet died. When did it die? If you know the cause, tell about it. Knowing the cause often helps children accept the death.

Remember that children's reactions to the death will differ depending on their relationship with the pet. If they were responsible for its care and had close daily contact, their reactions will be strongest. But even the strongest reactions may vary from anger to sadness to guilt—particularly if the care of the pet was their responsibility. They'll also have different reactions depending on previous experiences with loss or death, as well as their stage of development or level of understanding. If they don't understand the finality of death when it occurs, they will come to understand it as time goes by (the dog never returns) and will develop the mental abilities to realize that death is permanent.

Once you've acknowledged the pet's death, let the children take the next step. Listen to their comments and questions for clues to help you understand how significant the event is for them. Offer suggestions but don't force them or yourself into specific responses. For example, if the death doesn't seem terribly upsetting, you might say, "Would you like me to take care of burying Goldie for you, or would you like to help?" On the other hand, if the death is very upsetting, you might be more directive by saying, "What can we do to show how much we cared for Goldie?"

What if a pet is lost or missing instead of dead? You still have to deal with the circumstances directly and honestly. If you know when the pet left or what direction it headed, share this information with the children. Don't pretend the dog is missing when you know it is dead. But if you don't know it is dead, be honest about that too. It's OK to say, "I don't know if Fido just wandered off and got lost or got killed by a car."

Once you've shared what you know, allow children time to ask questions or share feelings. Be prepared for a variety of responses from disinterested to inconsolable. Honest communication builds the strongest foundation for further exploration of a situation and the range of emotions that may result.

As children share their responses with you, begin offering practical suggestions. Maybe you can conduct a neighborhood search, or call the animal shelter, or make "lost cat" posters for area bulletin boards. If it's too late at night, you may have to wait until morning to take further actions. If children are responding emotionally, acknowledge that it may be difficult to sleep but explain that the search will be safer and easier in daylight.

It is important to let the children be as actively involved as possible. Involvement can mean doing something or just being included in knowing all the facts. Whatever form it takes, involvement is one of the keys to coping effectively with loss and death.

If it turns out that the pet is dead, children may want to have a funeral and/or a burial. When it's their choice, this is a good idea. If you're in a rural area with plenty of open spaces this probably won't create any problems. If you're in an urban area, space or regulations may rule out a burial. A goldfish or hamster is easy to bury because it doesn't require a large space or a deep grave. But a cat or dog is more difficult. You may need to suggest that the veterinarian cremate your pet (if this fits your belief system). Then you can have a funeral/memorial service but no burial.

Whenever possible, let children decide how the service will take place. If they ask you a question about the burial or ceremony, try to respond with choices. Sometimes you may have to limit the children's options based on what you're willing, able or allowed to do. You may have city regulations that must be followed, or personal time constraints.

But whenever possible, give the children choices. For example, "One of you could carry the box with Goldie in it, or we could put it in the wagon and pull it out to the grave site." Or, "We could bury Rusty back by the fence, or we could take him to the vet and ask the vet to cremate him for us."

Responding to a Loss or a Death _____ 115

If you're at home and you feel that a prayer is important, say one. If you're at school where children bring ideas from different cultures and religions, let them mix up their rituals in whatever ways they choose. The whole purpose of the activity is for the children to express their reaction to the death, honor the dead pet and make the death real by making a physical and/or verbal good-bye.

Remember that initial urge to simply replace the pet? You know it shouldn't be done secretly. Should it be done at all? This will be a familiar answer: whenever you can, let the children decide. When they ask for a new hamster, that's a good time to discuss it. You may have to explain that a new pet won't be possible due to space or money. Or you may discuss what type of pet to get and where to get it.

In general, getting a new pet immediately is not a good idea, because this might lead the child to believe that one being can be replaced by another. "Does that mean *I* can be replaced?" This is uncomfortable and possibly frightening. Make sure children understand that a new pet may be fun and we'll learn to love it, but the new pet won't be the same as Rusty, and we won't care for Rusty any less.

When a Grandparent Dies

If children are told the facts about the death of a grandparent, then listened to and comforted at home, they may be able to cope with their feelings well enough so that teachers never know about the death. This is especially possible if the grandparent didn't live nearby or the child had only a distant or occasional relationship with the grandparent.

But if the child was raised by the grandparent or had a similar close relationship, the child's responses are likely to occur at home *and* at school. In both settings children want their feelings to be respected and accepted. Listen carefully, then share your own feelings and/or beliefs.

If you're talking to children at home you may have all the facts needed to share with the children. If you're talking to children at school you may not know the facts. In that case you may be responding to questions from the children to help them understand facts they've been told, or help them decide what questions they want to ask when they get home. You might begin by asking children what they know and/or feel about the death.

When a Teacher or Public Figure Dies

When a teacher or a public figure dies, younger children may display their self-centeredness by completely ignoring the event. Even though the whole community may be talking about it, if the children didn't really know the person who died, they may go on with their daily routines unaffected. However, if their teacher dies (or their neighbor, the mayor) they may need help coping with the event.

Children's concerns might sound like these: "Who will be our new teacher?" "Will our new teacher take us to the fire department next Friday like we planned?" "I wish I wasn't so mean to Mr. Smith before he died." "I hope our next teacher is more fun than Miss Jones. I never liked her." "Why is Billy still so sad? Mr. Smith died a long time ago and I like Miss Goodman better anyway."

Depending on the child's perspective, he or she may need to be reassured that new routines can be learned and that any feelings—except "guilty"—are acceptable. Explain that some things like lunchtime and P.E. will be the same as before, but the new teacher may have a different way of doing show and tell or assigning homework. Let children know what you know and help them learn ways of finding out new information for themselves. You might suggest that being nice to teachers is important, but liking teachers is not necessary. It's also OK if one child's opinion or perspective is different from another's. Children's individual relationships with the teacher were different; their responses will be different too.

When the person who dies is a public person, the school, neighborhood and media will be talking about the death. In these circumstances children often overhear more than they can understand. Be aware when children are listening. Make sure you use honest and direct language as described in Chapter 4. Be sure the children have an opportunity to ask questions so you can be sure of how much they understand, and whether they have all the information they need.

If you want to discuss any aspect of the death that might cause unnecessary fear or confusion for children, have your discussion away from the children. Remember that although we don't want to hide the death from children, we also don't want to give them more information than they can cope with or understand.

If the death is due to AIDS you may discuss the cause and possibly lead into a discussion about prevention. But there is no need to discuss the details of the person's physical deterioration. Fear of AIDS as a deadly disease is enough reality. Fear of the symptoms and side-effects isn't necessary to understanding, coping with and readjusting after the death.

When a public figure dies, communities often organize a public memorial. This brings the death to the attention of more people and involves more people in the memorial rituals—including children. These are excellent opportunities for children to witness the variety of responses (both emotional and practical) that people have related to death.

A school may plant a memorial tree or have a memorial service or time of silence to honor a teacher. Communities may organize the ringing of all church bells in unison at the beginning of the funeral. Newspapers may print eulogies written by residents to honor community philanthropists or leaders. When you're considering your own participation in these events, remember to offer a role to your children.

Children who are interested in or need to be involved in these grieving and memorial rituals can participate in any of the activities listed above. When children are strongly affected, they may have specific ideas of their own about how they want to participate. Since children often don't feel bound by social conventions, they may provide fresh insights and excellent suggestions.

Because the death of a public figure affects so many people in one community, the event may remain in people's minds longer than the death of a lesser-known person. As children work to learn the expectations of a new teacher, they come across daily reminders of the dead teacher. Each time a routine is changed, they're reminded of how it used to be. Continue listening and watching for clues to children's coping abilities as long as needed. Encourage positive coping skills like reminiscing over pictures or stories. And get additional help if you note reactions that you think might harm the child's development—extended lack of interest in other activities or people, or feelings of guilt, for example.

When a Parent Dies

When a parent dies a child's perspective probably centers on his or her own security. Your role as the surviving parent, relative, teacher or friend is to provide as much reassurance as possible. Don't tell children everything will be OK—of course things won't be OK without their parent. But do tell them who will fix their breakfast, or who will take them to baseball practice, or who will stay home with them when they are sick or read them a bedtime story.

Let them know that you understand it won't be the same, but that they will be taken care of as well as possible. Even when you don't have an answer, remember that the truth is more reassuring than false hope that can backfire. When you don't know an answer, offer to find out, or help them find out, or promise to tell them whenever you find out. This allows children to feel included as much as possible.

What if the child/parent relationship was not a warm, supportive, healthy one? What if it was abusive? The same security issues usually arise. Since young children often don't know there is another way of life (i.e., not abusive), they think everyone has a similar lifestyle. They still love their parent(s) and look to them for security.

In most cases, your responses will be the same, regardless of the quality of the parent/child relationship. In some cases, however, older children may feel guilty or relieved about the death of an abusive parent. When these emotions are observed or heard, consider professional support. These are long-term, complex relationships that won't be completely resolved by comfort and teaching.

Within the home, death of a parent must be acknowledged immediately. If it's not a sudden death, it's even better to begin talking about the death before it happens. Acknowledge death by sharing honest facts, beliefs and feelings. Facts help children accept reality, while beliefs and feelings help them express, explore and grieve for the loss.

At school or church it may be tempting to avoid discussion about the death of a child's parent. But you're not bringing up the subject of death in this case—you're all thinking about it anyway. What you are doing is acknowledging the importance of the loss and providing some support and a role model to help children learn to cope with realities.

This can be a time of additional bonding for the surviving parent and children. Take this opportunity to include the children in as many activities and decisions as you can. It will not be easy, but all difficult tasks are made easier when shared with a loved one. If you're concerned about whether children should go with you to choose a gravestone, consider asking the children if they'd like to go or help. If this seems too difficult, tell children why you have to go alone. Then make sure they have caring adults and a comfortable place to wait for your return.

Regarding the funeral or other ceremonies, it is more important for children to attend when it is their own parent who has died. You need to push yourself to either handle the children's needs, or to find someone you and your children trust to be their comforter. Children should be encouraged but not forced to attend services. Force just adds another level of stress that is unnecessary.

While offering a choice, adults can still encourage children to attend by describing the supportive benefits, by assuring children that they will be cared for during the process, or simply by stating that you will feel better if the children you love are with you.

If the funeral is for a friend's parent, attending funeral services is less critical to children's acceptance of finality. The death may be further removed and children can be offered a choice with less direction from adults. The closer the relationship, the greater the need for the finality and support provided by death-related ceremonies.

Ceremonies are usually over in a few days. But children have a long-range task in adjusting to life without a parent. They are likely to find daily reminders of the parent throughout the home and their routines. Each daily reminder, regardless of size or significance, constitutes a specific loss which needs to be acknowledged directly and honestly just as the death itself was.

As you continue to deal with each loss, be alert to children's ongoing need for support and your own need for personal support and help with your children. As you teach children to ask for support and express their feelings, remember to follow your own advice. Seek assistance for yourself too. Ask your friends and relatives to help keep an eye on the children's readjustment. Your eyes may be too clouded with your own grieving to see your children's needs clearly.

In addition to daily reminders, each holiday or special occasion may renew the depth of the loss. Holiday traditions are a powerful part of children's sense of security. It is difficult to let go of the comfort of the old traditions and adjust to or develop new traditions.

Although we want children to get on with their new life without a parent, we can't expect them to do it easily. Use holidays to remember old ways. Remember the way Mom used to hide the birthday cake so it would be a surprise? or the way Dad always sang when he put on the holiday lights? Talk to the children to see if they want to keep up some of the old practices or leave them as special memories. They may want everyone to sing as the lights are put on, in honor of Dad. Or they may not want singing because it interferes with their pleasant memories.

Different children find comfort in different ways, just as adults do. The appropriate response is the one that most helps the particular child.

If you find that children aren't getting on with celebrating or playing or learning or loving in their lives, consider professional counseling. Don't let the death of a parent prevent a healthy life for a child. And don't blame yourself for a child's inability to readjust. When the steps you've taken seem inadequate, or when a child stops growing and developing, it is a time to take positive action, not to blame.

In the case of an abusive parent's death, once children find a new sense of security without the abusive parent, they may begin to confront their feelings about the abuse. They may realize that they actually feel better without the parent in their lives. The complexity and depth of these awakenings require more than a supportive environment. You haven't failed unless you fail to be concerned about the children's welfare; continue to seek professional help for them.

When a Child Dies

An elderly person's death fits with our view of the natural order of things; a child's death does not. This is not just an adult perspective. Even children who have come a long way toward understanding that death is final, unavoidable and inevitable still believe that it happens to grownups, not children. This concept is one of the last to develop in children.

Developmentally, this means children aren't really ready to conceive of their own deaths. Then what happens to a child's perspective when another child dies? Some children will totally block out the event. They will refuse to think about it. This may be a mechanism for self-preservation; the child may simply be unable to handle the information at this time.

Other children will make an instant jump into a new and frightening level of awareness—that death is *personal*. Although they weren't developmentally ready to take in this information, real-life circumstances have forced them to be more grown-up. As a result, the greatest degree of support may be needed when another child dies.

With supportive adults in their lives, children can learn to cope with their new knowledge and feelings. It will take some longer than others, but they will learn. As with other deaths, the closeness of the relationship between the surviving child and the one who died will affect the way the child deals with the death.

Although children can't be pushed into acceptance and understanding of the death of another child, the circumstances must be dealt with directly and honestly. Be open to children's questions and concerns; provide answers and support as they follow their own pace toward understanding.

Because of children's developmental level and their emotional involvement, it may take longer to accept the death of a child than any other death. You can help by acknowledging the death and clarifying the circumstance of the death.

It is important to help children see how they are different from the child who died and also how they are similar. For example, if a child dies of leukemia and the children you are working with are not cancer patients, you can point out your children's health as a difference in this particular situation. If a child is hit by a car, or dies from an overdose of drugs, use this as a teaching opportunity in addition to providing emotional support to the children.

Gently, over time, you can help children understand. Help them find ways to be involved, such as participating in a school memorial or writing notes to the parents of the child who died. Although some parents will reject overtures from other children attempting to console them, others will be touched and comforted by the children's actions. Prepare the children for possible negative reactions from the parents. But remember that the purpose of the activity is to help the *children* work through their feelings. If these are true gestures from the hearts of the children, they are likely to be accepted as such.

There are some situations where children are likely to need professional help in adjusting to the death of another child: if they witness an accidental death; if the death is violent; if children shared an accident or traumatic event and some died while some lived. Also, if the similarities between the child who died and the surviving children are significant, children may be too fearful to cope with the death without assistance from trained professionals. Don't forget that they'll still need your support in addition to whatever professional support they receive.

As time goes by, you can help just by sharing children's memories. Listen to their stories, help them care for a keepsake item, or watch the annual budding of the memorial tree together. Remember not to suggest that new friends take the place of old ones. We don't *replace* human beings in our lives. But we can encourage children to enjoy new friendships in addition to remembering the old one.

When the Death Is Sudden and Violent

Children are bombarded on a daily basis with images of sudden, violent death—fatal automobile crashes, drive-by shootings, suicides and homicides—through newspapers, television, movies and other media. Children can become aware of these kinds of deaths through planned activities like those described in Chapter 5. None of these experiences, however, can ever prepare them for the sudden death of a loved one or the violent death of someone they have known.

Children must go through the same stages of grief when dealing with these tragic sudden deaths: denial, anger, bargaining, depression and acceptance. However, they also experience tremendous shock with no time to prepare or adjust. They may need more help, guidance and time to deal with an unexpected death, particularly if it was violent. Like adults, children may go through a period of emotional numbness followed by feelings of resentment, anger, loneliness, guilt, hurt, blame and sadness.

Violent death may also bring about feelings of anxiety and fear for safety. A drive-by shooting, a rape or a drug overdose may confirm a child's perceptions about dangers in the neighborhood. A suicide committed by a classmate may confirm a child's perceptions that his or her future is hopeless and that the only way to deal with that hopelessness is to take one's own life. The brutal death of three friends in an automobile crash may confirm a young child's fear of riding to the supermarket with his or her parents.

As soon as possible, reassure children that they are safe. Parents and teachers can help children deal with violent deaths by providing them with understanding, comfort and accurate information. Remember, what you say and how you say it will depend on the child's developmental stage.

Explain what happened, but don't feel it necessary to give a graphic description. Make sure the information is accurate. In most cases, when a violent death occurs, inaccurate rumors lead to unnecessary panic and anxiety. If the deceased was a student or teacher in the child's school, acknowledge the death and be sensitive to the child's need to talk about it.

Some schools have a crisis response system to respond to the death of a student or staff member. This organized response often enables students and staff to return to emotional normality sooner. Although school plans may vary from site to site, the primary purposes are to provide accurate information for all students and staff, to allay unnecessary fears by creating a safe, secure environment, and to provide emotional support for those most closely associated with the person who died. The response system may include writing letters to parents and other community members, allowing teachers and students to attend funeral services, doing something for the immediate family, providing small-group counseling for students and staff, and planning a school memorial.

Are You Sad Too?

Chapter 7

Using Children's Literature to Teach About Death

Even when children are developmentally able to think about abstract concepts, "hands on" activities still may make the greatest impact. In the case of death education, where real examples can't be simulated, the next best option for parents and teachers is to use literature. Children's literature can provide situations or scenarios likely to elicit reactions similar to what might occur in a real-life experience.

This chapter offers suggestions for selecting appropriate children's literature and using it effectively, followed by specific examples of children's stories and ways to use them.

Choosing a Book

When choosing literature for use in death education, think about the following points:

- ❧ the appropriate developmental level
- ❧ whether you want fiction or nonfiction
- ❧ what approach you want the story to take
- ❧ whether you want a focused or comprehensive story

Select an Age-Appropriate Book

Remember to consider the developmental level of the children in regard to their understanding of death. Because of our societal taboos, this level may be lower than their developmental level in, for instance, math or science. Preview a book by trying to think from the child's perspective as you read it. Then prepare to bring the discussion level up or down depending on the responses you will receive from the children.

For purposes of this chapter, books are recommended for just two general stages: children ages three through five and those ages six through eight. Children age nine and over may be reading and choosing books on their own. They can benefit from any of the books recommended for the six-through-eight stage.

There really are no books aimed at children under three. When these youngest children experience a death, they are likely to jump ahead developmentally with regard to understanding it. When death is a reality in their lives you'll be able to use some of the books for three through five year olds to help comfort and teach them. Stories that are simplest, or are most like the actual situation, will work best.

Fiction or Nonfiction?

Fiction will work best in most situations. Whether you're presenting a planned classroom unit on death education, or preparing a child for an expected death in the family, using a fictional story to develop scenarios will often draw out children's feelings, knowledge and/or beliefs.

A story will help children cope with a death experience if it shows the range of common feelings and responses to help children feel more "normal" or comfortable with their own reactions. The last part of this chapter suggests fictional stories that highlight some useful death education concepts.

Nonfiction books on death and dying are probably more useful for adults than for children. Because these books often focus only on technical details, children who are less experienced with the concept of death may find this somewhat detached approach too harsh or blunt. Although emotions may be discussed, they are often presented as generic or abstract instead of personal and meaningful. In most cases, a more sympathetic (personal, human, real-life, realistic) approach will be desirable, even when the child's questions focus on factual details.

In addition, nonfiction books about death tend to cover too much material. They present too many steps for children to understand at one time. Many nonfiction books can be useful to adults, however, by providing background material on the subject of death at varying levels of detail. They also provide excellent models for direct language to be used with children at different levels.

Examples of nonfiction books for the three-through-five stage:

- *A Look at Death,* by Rebecca Anders
- *Sunny: The Death of a Pet,* by Judith E. Greenberg and Helen H. Carey
- *When a Pet Dies,* by Fred Rogers

Examples for the six-through-eight stage:

- *When People Die,* by Joanne E. Bernstein and Stephen V. Gullo
- *Death and Dying,* by Jean Knox
- *When Someone You Love Dies,* by Linda L. Potter

These books and others are listed in the Suggested Readings section at the back of this book.

Consider the Book's Approach

Authors of children's books approach the subject of death in various ways. Death may be the main theme of the book, or it may be a secondary theme—with less emphasis placed on it. Some books take a natural or biological approach to the subject of death, while others use metaphors or fantasy. When a book deals directly with a specific death, some authors have chosen to write about the death of a grandparent while others write about the death of a parent, child or pet.

When you're choosing a book to read to children, consider which approach will be most helpful. You may precede a death education unit with a story in which death is a secondary theme. This format may help you judge the children's knowledge and emotional responses to the subject while helping you plan lessons directed more accurately at your children's level of understanding. The books referred to in this chapter all have death as the primary theme.

Books taking a natural or biological approach to death typically use the seasons of nature to describe the natural flow of life and death. An author will emphasize the fact that death is a natural and necessary part of life. For the three-through-five stage, the book *Lifetimes: The Beautiful Way to Explain Death to Children* (Mellonie and Ingpen, 1983) tells this story simply and directly.

For the six-through-eight stage, *The Fall of Freddie the Leaf* (Buscaglia, 1982) and *Death Is Natural* (Pringle, 1977) teach this lesson well. Buscaglia tells the story of Freddie, a leaf with lifelike qualities and thoughts. This is a popular and easy-to-find book with a clever, fun-to-read, positive attitude toward death. Adults may have to clarify some of the facts and metaphors used. Dying is referred to as changing homes, not hurting, and being more comfortable. In the context of the book these all make sense to an adult reader, but children may need some help understanding. The descriptions of afterlife, while positive and interesting, may require some interpretation for children. Pringle presents general feelings and beliefs about death in an ecological-primer style. Life cycles, nature's balance and natural selection are emphasized. Books with this approach can be used effectively to initiate general discussion about death.

Although metaphors, like the dead body being nourishment for new growth, often are difficult for children to understand before age nine, some authors use them rather effectively. Before you use such a metaphorical story you should be very familiar with the abilities of your

Are You Sad Too?

children, and very comfortable personally with the specific metaphor used. If you are unsure about a story, either avoid using it or spend sufficient time discussing the metaphor to clarify its meaning for the children. If you think your children will enjoy and/or understand this kind of story, the following books are good examples:

- *First Snow,* by Helen Coutant
- *Annie and the Old One,* by Miska Miles
- *The Last Leaf,* by O. Henry

Sometimes authors write about a specific death experience. When you are working with children who are currently experiencing a death, choose a children's story in which the real experience and the story experience are similar. If you want to discuss the death of a pet, here are some examples:

- *The Accident,* by Carol Carrick
- *Mustard,* by Charlotte Graeber
- *Better with Two,* by Barbara M. Joosse
- *Goodbye, Max,* by Holly Keller
- *Whiskers Once and Always,* by Doris Orgel
- *Growing Time,* by Sandol S. Warburg

These books deal with the death of a grandparent:

- *My Grandpa Died Today,* by Joan Fassler
- *Grandpa's Slide Show,* by Deborah Gould
- *Why Did Grandpa Die?* by Barbara S. Hazen
- *My Grandmother Died—But I Won't Forget Her,* by Bernice Hogan
- *Why Did Grandma Die?* by Trudy Madler
- *Bubby, Me and Memories,* by Barbara Pomerantz

- *When Grandpa Died,* by Margaret Stevens
- *My Grandson Lew,* by Charlotte Zolotow

These books are about the death of a parent or teacher:

- *Its Okay to Cry,* by L. C. Anderson
- *Everett Anderson's Goodbye,* by Lucille Clifton
- *Z's Gift,* by Neal Starkman

And these stories deal with the death of a child:

- *I Had a Friend Named Peter: Talking to Children About the Death of a Friend,* by Janice Cohn
- *The Magic Moth,* by Virginia Lee
- *We Remember Philip,* by Norma Simon
- *The Saddest Time—Part Two,* by Norma Simon
- *A Taste of Blackberries,* by Doris B. Smith

Think About the Focus of the Book

Your last consideration when choosing a book for children is whether you want a story that is focused on a specific death education concept or whether you want a story that covers the concepts comprehensively. If you already know your children's abilities well, you might know that you need to focus on facts, feelings, beliefs or coping skills related to death. If you're fishing for clues to your children's understanding, you might decide to present a comprehensive story to see what area the children are most interested in, or where they need clarification.

In the rest of this chapter specific children's books with death themes are discussed. They are all fiction, with death as the main theme. The books are grouped according to the concept or teaching area being emphasized (facts, feelings, beliefs or coping skills), although there often are many other concepts included. The recommended age level is given for each book. The descriptions include a summary of the story followed by a discussion of the material that is particularly helpful or useful and the material that may need clarification. The list is not meant to be comprehensive.

Books That Emphasize Facts

When Grandpa Died
Margaret Stevens
Chicago: Children's Press, 1979
Ages 3 through 5

A little girl and her grandfather are good friends. They live in the same home and spend a lot of time together. When they find a dead bird, the girl describes it as cold and hard. They discuss possible causes for the bird's death but they don't know for sure. They put cotton around the bird and bury it in a box in the yard, and plant a flower to show where it is buried. Grandpa discusses the fact that death is natural and that all living things die sometime.

Then one day Grandpa gets very sick and after a while has to go to the hospital. Mom and Dad visit Grandpa every day, but eventually they come home crying and the girl is frightened. Then, when she's told that Grandpa is dead, she's angry at him for dying. She wears Grandpa's sweater and sits in his room to cry and comfort herself. Dad hugs her and tells her it's OK to cry. She says she's sad because she didn't get to say good-bye to Grandpa. So Dad tells her there will be a funeral for saying good-bye. Dad takes her to the funeral home to see the coffin, and the next day they attend the funeral. After a while the girl realizes that Grandpa won't ever come back, and that when her little sister grows up she'll have to tell her all about him.

The story focuses on the fact that death is final. It also refers to some causes of death and the physical qualities of the dead bird. The helping rituals of funerals are described, and both the bird and Grandpa have a coffin and a funeral. Although some books go into more detail, this would be a good introduction to the topic of death for very young children. It treats death matter-of-factly and answers some primary questions.

A Taste of Blackberries
Doris B. Smith
New York: HarperCollins, 1973
Ages 6 through 8

This story is told completely from a child's perspective. A boy tells about his relationship with his best friend and neighbor, Jamie, and what happens when Jamie dies. In the beginning, the two boys have many adventures together. One day when all the neighborhood children are helping a neighbor with yardwork, Jamie pokes a stick in a bees' nest and stirs up a swarm of bees. Because Jamie is always acting silly and dramatic, none of the children pay any attention when Jamie falls down. They all just run away from the bees. Later an ambulance comes for Jamie, but some of the children still suspect that Jamie is just acting to get attention as he always does. That evening, the main character's mother tells him Jamie died in the ambulance on the way to the hospital.

The children realistically express their disbelief that someone could die from a bee sting, or that Jamie could be dead. They are even jealous of his ride in the ambulance. As the reality sinks in, the boy begins to think about all the things he'll miss now that Jamie is dead. He still switches back and forth from pretending Jamie isn't dead to not being able to eat or play because of his grief. When his parents get ready to leave for the funeral home he panics and yells, "Wait for me!" The pretending is over.

The description of the death rituals begins with people going row by row to look into the open casket. The boy isn't sure whether he will look until he gets to the casket. Then he thinks, "If it was possible that Jamie knew what was going on, I wanted him to know that I was here, thinking about him." He describes all the people talking in whispers or crying. When one woman says Jamie looks as if he's asleep, the boy thinks, "He didn't look like he was asleep to me. Jamie slept bunched up. Jamie looked dead." At home, after the visitation, his parents offer comforting words and hugs.

The next day is the funeral. As the boy spends some quiet time thinking about Jamie and the funeral, a neighbor joins him. The boy asks, "Why did he have to die?" and "What's it like to be dead?" The neighbor replies, "One of the hardest things we have to learn is that some questions do not have answers." The boy feels that this makes more sense than "junk about God needing angels." His mother tells him it won't help Jamie for him not to eat, but he feels that he shouldn't eat until after the funeral. "Somehow," he says, "I couldn't let things be the same."

The events of the afternoon are described fully from the child's perspective, including the funeral car, funeral parlor chapel, music, flowers, talking and reading the Bible, funeral procession, cemetery, "Jamie's hole" and the graveside service.

In the last chapter the boy remembers picking blackberries with Jamie. He decides to pick an extra bucket of berries for Jamie's mother. As he picks, he carries on a conversation with himself, the berries, and sometimes with Jamie. He follows the rules he and Jamie had had about not eating any berries before the picking was done. When he finally eats a berry he thinks about Jamie: "Do you remember the taste of blackberries?" When he delivers the berries to Jamie's mother he is uncomfortable about reminding her of Jamie. But after they talk briefly, the boy says that "Joy burst within me and I blinked the stinging out of my eyes. I knew she understood everything I wanted to tell her." He is no longer ashamed about the other children playing when Jamie is dead—he is able to join them.

There are many feelings and beliefs expressed in this story. But one of its strengths is the telling of the full story, realistically, from a boy's perspective. It starts with the relationship between the boys, then the facts of the accident and a description of the ambulance taking Jamie from his house. The boy's feelings are shown as varied, opposite and continually changing as he prepares for the funeral. But once he makes the decision to attend the funeral the vacillating and pretending ends with acknowledging the finality of the death of his best friend.

The rituals from visitation to graveside service are described clearly and with good detail, again focusing on the boy's perspective. He expresses his appreciation of a neighbor who answers his questions honestly and directly. When the rituals are over, the boy is shown getting back to his routine life, including reinstating his relationship with Jamie's mother and his other friends. This is an excellent book with a realistic and complete view of what it's like when a friend dies—the child's perspective is accurately and sensitively presented.

Books That Emphasize Feelings

Everett Anderson's Goodbye
Lucille Clifton
New York: Holt, Rinehart and Winston, 1983
Ages 3 through 5

Everett Anderson is a young boy who goes through the five stages of grieving as he learns to accept his father's death. Each of the short chapters addresses one of the stages of dealing with death. The stages are very concisely phrased, using the child's perspective. The boy denies, gets angry, bargains, gets depressed and finally accepts his father's death. Then he learns how to keep part of his father close, by using his memories.

The emotions of the characters are captured in realistic sketches which are quite powerful. The story focuses on acceptance of all the different stages and feelings and ends with a very hopeful positive attitude toward accepting death in our lives. Very young children will be able to understand this book, and older children will be moved to experience new levels of empathy and awareness.

Goodbye, Max
Holly Keller
New York: Greenwillow Books, 1987
Ages 3 through 5

This story begins with Ben and his dad discussing their dead pet, Max. Ben remembers Max as a good friend. When Dad suggests that a new dog can be a friend, too, Ben shakes his head and says, "Not like Max." Later when a new puppy is offered, Ben gets angry and doesn't want anything to do with the "ugly" puppy. Ben's friend Zach asks him to come out and play, but Ben stays in his room remembering Max's death. When it's time for Ben to take care of his paper route, Zach goes along and helps with the papers. After a while both boys talk about missing Max. Ben sits on the curb and cries; Zach joins him until they "can cry no more." As the boys are walking home they stop for a minute to look at Max's gravestone. At home Ben picks up the new puppy and decides it's time to name him.

This book is clear, simple, honest and direct. It describes a variety of feelings that are "normal" in grieving children. Ben protests when his father suggests that a new puppy would be as good as Max. He is angry with the doctor for not making Max well, and he's angry at his mother for making him go to school on the day that Max was very sick and died.

Ben moves from disbelief to acceptance and finds out how caring friends and going on with daily routines can help you feel a little better. The burial and gravestone are referred to only briefly, but the stone is emphasized as something that helps Ben remember Max. Although replacing a pet is not recommended, many well-meaning adults try this approach. This story shows children that it's not unusual to be angry and refuse another pet. It also shows that it's OK to say how you feel, and to change your mind later when you're ready to start a new relationship.

The Accident
Carol Carrick
New York: Seabury Press, 1976
Ages 6 through 8

Christopher and his dog, Bodger, are best friends. One night they're out taking a walk along the road. Christopher hears a truck coming and calls Bodger to cross the road to be with him. Bodger waits too long, then runs into the road. The truck swerves but can't avoid hitting Bodger. Christopher's parents arrive at the accident, and his father talks with the truck driver. Christopher is disappointed with his father because he can't change the situation. Christopher thinks his father doesn't care about Bodger because he isn't mad at the driver. The driver is sympathetic and offers a new puppy. But Christopher only wants Bodger.

That night at home Christopher relives the accident over and over in his mind. He pretends the truck missed, that he didn't call Bodger, that they had stayed home—but it always ends with Bodger dead. The next morning Christopher almost forgets about the accident until he sees Bodger's dishes missing from their usual place. Dad offers a fishing trip and Mom offers French toast, but Christopher doesn't want anything.

He goes out to sit on the steps and think about Bodger. Dad joins him. At first they're quiet, then Christopher asks, "What did you do with Bodger?" When Dad tells Christopher he buried Bodger by the brook, Christopher is angry at not being included and leaves the house for a walk. When he calms down a little, he returns home and Dad says, "Why don't we take the canoe along the shore to find a nice stone to mark Bodger's grave?"

During the search for the perfect stone, Christopher becomes excited about the project. When they place the stone on Bodger's grave Christopher and his Dad remember stories about Bodger that make them laugh. Their laughing turns into crying which "felt good this time." Dad reaches out and Christopher allows his dad to comfort him.

The emotions expressed from the child's perspective are excellent examples of the five stages in the grieving process. And the feelings expressed go beyond the five stages into embarrassment, excitement, laughter, fear and confusion. In addition to a depth of emotion, the book very positively shows parents being accepting of the child's feelings, allowing him time to work through even the ugly ones like "I ought to run him [the driver] over with a truck."

The parents also share their feelings with their son and help him find a way to get involved in commemorating the dead pet. Some children may react to the loss associated with the realization that parents can't always make things better. Children can relate to this story because it is realistic and presents the child's perspective directly and honestly.

Books That Emphasize Beliefs

Better with Two
Barbara M. Joosse
Singapore: HarperCollins, 1988
Ages 3 through 5

Mrs. Brady and her dog Max are friends and neighbors of Laura's. One day Laura notices Mrs. Brady sitting on the porch swing without Max. When Mrs. Brady tells Laura that Max died, Laura remembers Max's plaid coat, his fuzzy feel—and then she cries. Her mother hugs her until she's done crying, then says, "Crying is better with two."

Laura thinks Mrs. Brady continues to look lonely and sad. She also notices that the swing rocks crooked without Max in the swing with Mrs. Brady. Laura brings Mrs. Brady flowers, a drawing and a china dog to help cheer her up, but Mrs. Brady is still sad. At last, Laura comes up with another idea to help Mrs. Brady's sadness. She sits on Mrs. Brady's swing so it will go straight. When Mrs. Brady smiles a bit, Laura thinks, "Like crying, swinging is better with two."

This very simple story strongly illustrates the belief that people need other people to comfort them, that the caring of others is helpful, and that the person doing the comforting also feels better for having helped. The mother gives the child a model which the child then uses to help her friend. This is a very empowering story for children because the main character, Laura, is shown being involved and quite useful. Although it seems simple on the surface, this story brings out meaningful ways to approach grief positively and learn to think about other people's sadness. And it's done in a way that even very young children can understand.

Growing Time
Sandol S. Warburg
Boston: Houghton Mifflin, 1969
Ages 6 through 8

Jamie and his dog, King, live in a big country house with an orchard. King is very, very old now and sleeps most of the time. He doesn't play anymore, his legs hurt and his teeth are nearly gone. "The time of King's life is nearly over now." One morning Mother tells Jamie that King is dead. Jamie cries and questions "Why?" and "Where is he?" Jamie sees tears in his mother's eyes too as they talk for a long time. Mother shares her beliefs with Jamie, saying King is better off now and he doesn't hurt anymore. She acknowledges that the loss hurts very badly and won't stop hurting right away.

Later Jamie goes outside to talk with Uncle John. Uncle John clarifies that *gone* and *dead* are not the same thing; then he asks Jamie if he really knows what *dead* is. Uncle John reminds Jamie that he has seen dead leaves fall and flowers blossoming and then dying. When Jamie asks what will happen to King, his uncle explains that King's body will melt away into the ground and become part of the earth. Jamie says he wanted King to live a long time, until Jamie was grown up. But Uncle John explains that King had to live his own time, not Jamie's. Then

Uncle John invites Jamie to help him in the garden, telling him, "It's good to work when we're sorrowing."

When Jamie goes back inside, he sits quietly beside Granny for the afternoon. He pretends to play with a truck but he's really thinking of King. When he tells Granny that he wants King to come back, she asks where he thinks King has gone. Jamie says, "Under apple trees where Uncle John buried him." Granny says, "What's buried is nothing to King anymore." She says there's more to King than four tired legs, yellow fur and a sore mouth with no teeth. But according to Uncle John his spirit is gone. Granny says this is true, but asks where it has gone: "Has King's spirit got no home to come to anymore?"

When Jamie says that of course King's home is with him, Granny says that's where King's been all afternoon, right there with the two of them. Granny tells Jamie that with age you learn to count on your heart more than your eyes. She says, "So remember this, child, the spirit of something you really love can never die. It lives in your heart. It belongs to you always, it is your treasure."

That evening, Mom and Dad bring home a new puppy. It just makes Jamie feel worse about King and he rejects the new puppy. His father apologizes to him and says the dog doesn't have to stay. He tells Jamie that the decision is completely up to him. During the night Jamie dreams a lot, ending with a thumping which makes him smile as he remembers King's thumping tail on the kitchen floor. When he wakes, he finds the puppy in a mess, crying and shivering. Jamie picks up the puppy, comforts him, and begins to think about the future with the new puppy.

This is a story of a very warm and supportive family. The adults ask for Jamie's feelings and beliefs and then share their own feelings and beliefs with him. Between his mother, father, granny and Uncle John, Jamie is taught the family's belief system. If these beliefs differ significantly from your own, it may not be a good story for you to use. On the other hand, you may decide to use this book along with one showing different beliefs and discuss the differences. If you agree with these beliefs, however, this is a wonderful book that brings out many important concepts about death in a very clear and sensitive manner.

Books That Emphasize Coping Skills

The Saddest Time—Part Two
Norma Simon
Niles, IL: Albert Whitman and Company, 1986
Ages 3 through 5

This book has three short stories in it. The second story begins with a school assembly where the principal is telling the children that their classmate Teddy Baker died yesterday. The students are told that Teddy rode his bike into a street and was hit by a car. He died in the ambulance on the way to the hospital. His father and mother were with him. The principal also talks about eight years old being too young to die and wishing the accident had never happened.

After the assembly the students return to their classrooms. The students in Mr. Grady's room see Teddy's empty desk and begin talking about Teddy. They remember pleasant and unpleasant things about him; the teacher is accepting of all their comments. Then one student says that his parents are writing a letter to Teddy's parents and asks if the class can do that too. Mr. Grady thinks it's a good idea, and the children begin reminiscing again to think of things to write in their letters. "The more they talked, the more they remembered. They hoped their letters would make his mother and father know how much they missed their friend Teddy Baker."

This is a very short story that directly and honestly tells the facts about the accident and the various feelings children have. It gives a model for action. The teacher is shown letting the children take the initiative about what to do to show their feelings. The reactions of the children are realistic and varied, which will help readers understand and relate to the situation. You will want to remind your children that these are just *some* of the feelings and reactions that people have in response to death. But this story is a very good starting point for bringing out the feelings and ideas of very young children.

We Remember Philip
Norma Simon
Niles, IL: Albert Whitman and Company, 1979
Ages 6 through 8

In this story a teacher's son dies in a rock-climbing accident. The adults help the students show that they care by arranging a memorial tree planting. The children also get involved by asking parents for pictures that the other teachers use to prepare a slide show at school for a memorial. Finally, the children send sympathy cards and letters to the teacher, Mr. Hall, and his wife.

This book is a great example of the sympathetic and empathetic capacity of children and their need to help others. It is a good model to use in showing various ways children, adults and even whole communities can get involved in memorials and help grieving family members. The methods used by the characters in the book could be copied or they could start children and adults brainstorming about the best ways to memorialize a particular person in the community. This story is an excellent demonstration of teachers taking positive action when a death occurs.

&a &a &a

One final book deserves special attention as a comprehensive story. It covers all the major death education concepts in a positive and helpful manner. It could be used for almost any children under ten simply by varying the depth of the follow-up discussion and activities. Before the children's story is read, you should read the introduction, in which the author writes to parents answering many frequently asked questions related to teaching children about death. You'll then be well prepared to use the contents of the story to teach your children. Because of the intensity of this book, and the fact that a child dies, you are not likely to use it as an introduction to death education. You will want to do some simpler activities first. However, if a child in your school or community dies, children can benefit from this story immediately.

I Had a Friend Named Peter:
Talking to Children About the Death of a Friend
Janice Cohn
New York: William Morrow and Company, 1987
Ages 3 through 5 and 6 through 8

In this story, Betsy and Peter are good friends. When Peter is hit by a car and dies, Betsy's parents begin by explaining the details of his accident. They make sure that Betsy understands what *dead* really means. They answer all her questions directly and honestly while providing physical and verbal comfort. The morgue, funeral, and burial are all described clearly.

Betsy expresses anger—"It's not fair!"—and fear—"Can I die, too, like Peter?"—and experiences a stomachache and bad dream. Her parents share their feelings with Betsy too. When Betsy becomes too quiet, her parents assure her that there is "nothing so terrible that you cannot talk to us about it." But when to tell them and whether or not to attend the funeral are left up to Betsy to decide. When Betsy shares her concern that her argument with Peter caused his death, her parents assure her that wishes don't cause death; otherwise, Peter's parents could wish him back.

The next day at school, the children talk about their memories of Peter—the good and the bad. Then they decide to make pictures for themselves and for Peter's parents to help them remember Peter. The teacher ends the story by saying, "When people have lived—even for a short time, like Peter—they stay in the memories of the people who loved them, even after they have died. These memories don't ever go away; they last forever. And that is why Peter will never be forgotten."

Suggested Readings

Books for Adults

DeSpelder, L. A., and A. L. Strickland. 1983. *The Last Dance: Encountering Death and Dying.* Palo Alto, CA: Mayfield.

Eddy, J. M., and W. F. Alles. 1983. *Death Education.* St. Louis, MO: C. V. Mosby.

Grollman, E. 1967. *Explaining Death to Children.* Boston: Beacon.

Grollman, E. 1970. *Talking to Children About Death.* Boston: Beacon.

Hardt, D. V. 1979. *Death: The Final Frontier.* Englewood Cliffs, NJ: Prentice-Hall.

Kastenbaum, R., and R. Aisenberg. 1976. *The Psychology of Death.* New York: Springer.

Kubler-Ross, E. 1975. *Death: The Final Stage of Growth.* Englewood Cliffs, NJ: Prentice-Hall.

Kubler-Ross, E. 1969. *On Death and Dying.* New York: Macmillan.

Kubler-Ross, E. 1983. *On Children and Death.* New York: Macmillan.

Mendler, A. N. 1990. *Smiling at Yourself*. Santa Cruz, CA: ETR Associates.

Piaget, J. 1983. *The Child's Conception of the World*. Totowa, NJ: Rowman & Allanheld.

Russell, R. D., and C. O. Purdy. 1980. *Coping with Death and Dying*. Glenview, IL: Scott, Foresman.

Wass, H., and C. A. Corr. 1982. *Helping Children Cope with Death: Guidelines and Resources*. Washington, DC: Hemisphere.

Wolfelt, A. 1983. *Helping Children Cope with Grief*. Muncie, IN: Accelerated Development.

Books for Children

Anders, R. 1978. *A Look at Death*. Minneapolis, MN: Lerner Publications.

Anderson, L. C. 1979. *It's Okay to Cry*. Elgin, IL: Child's World.

Bernstein, J. E., and S. V. Gullo. 1977. *When People Die*. New York: Dutton.

Boulden, J. 1989. *Saying Goodbye*. Santa Rosa, CA: Author.

Buscaglia, L. 1982. *The Fall of Freddie the Leaf*. Thorofare, NJ: Slack.

Carrick, C. 1976. *The Accident*. New York: Seabury.

Clifton, L. 1983. *Everett Anderson's Goodbye*. New York: Holt, Rinehart & Winston.

Cohn, J. 1987. *I Had a Friend Named Peter: Talking to Children About the Death of a Friend*. New York: Morrow.

Coutant, H. 1974. *First Snow*. New York: Knopf.

Fassler, J. 1971. *My Grandpa Died Today*. New York: Human Sciences Press.

Gould, D. 1987. *Grandpa's Slide Show.* New York: Lothrop, Lee & Shepard.

Graeber, C. 1982. *Mustard.* New York: Bantam.

Greenberg, J. F., and H. H. Carey. 1986. *Sunny: The Death of a Pet.* New York: Franklin Watts.

Hazen, B. S. 1985. *Why Did Grandpa Die?* New York: Golden Books.

Hogan, B. 1983. *My Grandmother Died—But I Won't Forget Her.* Nashville, TN: Abingdon.

Joosse, B. M. 1988. *Better with Two.* Singapore: HarperCollins.

Keller, H. 1987. *Goodbye, Max.* New York: Greenwillow Books.

Knox, J. 1989. *Death and Dying.* New York: Chelsea House.

Lee, V. 1972. *The Magic Moth.* New York: Houghton Mifflin.

Madler, T. 1980. *Why Did Grandma Die?* Milwaukee, WI: Raintree.

Mellonie, B., and R. Ingpen. *Lifetimes: The Beautiful Way to Explain Death to Children.* New York: Bantam.

Miles, M. 1971. *Annie and the Old One.* Boston: Little, Brown.

O. Henry [W. S. Porter]. 1980. *The Last Leaf.* Mankato, MN: Creative Education.

Orgel, D. 1986. *Whiskers Once and Always.* New York: Viking Kestrel.

Pomerantz, B. 1983. *Bubby, Me and Memories.* New York: Union of American Hebrew Congregations.

Potter, L. L. 1979. *When Someone You Love Dies.* Lincoln, NE: Word Services.

Pringle, L. 1977. *Death Is Natural.* New York: Four Winds.

Rogers, F. 1988. *When a Pet Dies.* New York: Putnam.

Simon, N. 1979. *We Remember Philip.* Niles, IL: Albert Whitman.

Simon, N. 1986. *The Saddest Time.* Niles, IL: Albert Whitman.

Smith, D. B. 1973. *A Taste of Blackberries.* New York: HarperCollins.

Starkman, N. 1988. *Z's Gift.* Seattle, WA: Comprehensive Health Education Foundation.

Stevens, M. 1979. *When Grandpa Died.* Chicago: Children's Press.

Viorst, J. 1971. *The Tenth Good Thing About Barney.* New York: Macmillan.

Warburg, S. S. 1969. *Growing Time.* Boston: Houghton Mifflin.

Zolotow, C. 1974. *My Grandson Lew.* New York: HarperCollins.

References

Elkind, D. 1977. Life and death: Concepts and feelings in children. *Day Care and Early Childhood Education* 4 (3): 27–29, 39.

Furman, E. 1978. Helping children cope with death. *Young Children* 33 (4): 25–32.

Garanzini, M. J. 1987. Explaining death to children: The healing process. *Momentum* 18 (4): 30–32.

Ketchel, J. A. 1986. Helping the young child cope with death. *Day Care and Early Education* 14 (2): 24–27.

Ordal, C. C. 1980. Death as seen in books for young children. *Death Education* 4:223–236.

Pratt, C. C., J. Hare and C. Wright. 1987. Death and dying in early childhood education: Are educators prepared? *Education* 107:279–286.

Speece, M. W., and S. B. Brent. 1984. Children's understanding of death: A review of three components of a death concept. *Child Development* 55:1671–1686.

Wass, H., and C. A. Corr. 1982. *Helping children cope with death: Guidelines and resources.* Washington, DC: Hemisphere.

Wass, H., and J. Shaak. 1976. Helping children understand death through literature. *Childhood Education* 53:80-85.

Wenestam, C. G., and H. Wass. 1987. Swedish and U. S. children's thinking about death: A qualitative study and cross-cultural comparison. *Death Studies* 11:99-121.

Glossary

afterlife—An existence after death.

animism—Developmental stage when children attribute life to inanimate objects.

ashes—The remains of a dead body after cremation.

bereaved—State of suffering from the death of a loved one.

burial permit—Necessary document before burying a body.

casket—Box for burying dead body.

cemetery—Burial ground.

committal—Graveside service, including burial.

cremains—Ashes of cremated body.

cremation—Process used to reduce dead body to ashes by burning; may be an alternative to burial, or ashes may be buried.

crepe—Fabric worn or draped on a doorway as a sign of mourning.

crypt—Room used as a burial place, often underground.

death concepts—The way a person views death; these develop with increased understanding and include the following ideas:

avoidable—Can be escaped.

final—Not reversible.

impersonal—Can't happen to me or loved ones.

inevitable—Happens to everyone eventually.

personal—Can happen to me and my loved ones.

reversible—Changeable or temporary.

universal—Same as inevitable.

decomposition—Process of body decaying.

egocentrism—Developmental stage when children are unable to consider another's viewpoint.

embalming—Treatment of dead body to sanitize for viewing.

entombment—Burial in a mausoleum.

epitaph—Words written on a grave marker or monument.

eulogy—Speech of praise for a dead person.

euphemism—A less direct word substituted for one that is thought to be offensive.

funeral service—Ceremonies held for the dead before burial or cremation.

grave—A hole in the ground for burying a body.

grief—Extreme distress caused by bereavement.

hearse—Vehicle for taking the dead to the grave.

heaven—Religious term for the place blessed dead exist in communication with God.

hell—Religious term for the place where the damned exist in continual punishment.

immortality—Being exempt from death.

interment—Burial.

kaddish—Jewish prayer recited after death of a friend or relative.

last rites—Religious rituals to ease the transition from life to death.

magical thinking—Developmental stage when children believe objects and people have power to make other people do things.

mausoleum—Building for above-ground burials.

memorial service—Ceremony conducted after the burial or when the dead body is not present.

metaphor—A figure of speech in which one thing is spoken of as if it were another.

monument—Stone placed on a grave to remember the dead.

mortuary—Place where dead bodies are kept until burial.

mourning—Outward signs of grief or bereavement.

negative presentation of death—A view that is factually inaccurate; is not appropriate for the developmental level of the child; and/or creates unhealthy fears of life and death.

obituary—Notice of a person's death, usually in a newspaper or periodical.

pall—The heavy cloth draped over a casket.

pallbearer—A person who helps carry a casket at a funeral and burial.

positive presentation of death—A view that is factually accurate; is appropriate for the developmental level of the child; and/or creates a healthy understanding of death as a part of life.

reincarnation—Religious concept of rebirth into a new body or life form.

restoration—To make dead body look "lifelike" for viewing.

resurrection—Religious concept of rising from the dead.

resuscitation—Medical intervention to revive a person from apparent death or unconsciousness.

shiva—Jewish ritual of seven days of formal mourning after the funeral of a close relative.

shroud—The cloth or ritual garments a body is wrapped in when buried.

soul—Spiritual concept of the essence of an individual.

thanatology—The study of death and dying.

urn—A container used for keeping ashes of the dead.

vault—Concrete (or other strong material) as lining for a grave.

viewing—Same as visitation.

visitation—Physical display of a dead person at the funeral home or chapel.

wake—Christian watch over the dead body prior to the funeral, similar to visitation.

About the Authors

Dinah Seibert, MS, has made national presentations and published articles for health education professional organizations and is on the faculty in the College of Technical Careers at Southern Illinois University at Carbondale. Personal experience as parent, caregiver, and hospice advocate led her to further education and research in the area of children and death. She earned her master's degree in community health education from Southern Illinois University where her thesis research examined death themes in children's literature. Her teaching experience includes parenting, caring for aging parents, hospice care and organization, substance abuse, health promotion, health care management, professional development, technical writing and talking to children about death.

Judy C. Drolet, PhD, CHES, received her doctoral degree from the University of Oregon at Eugene. Much of her professional career has been directed toward the areas of sexuality education, death education, and professional preparation in health education. Since 1975 she has taught health education courses related to loss and death. Her teaching experience includes indepth courses in emotional/mental health, human growth and development, and death education. She has conducted and published research, presented papers at professional meetings, and directed graduate student research on death education with particular focus on experiences with children. She has been Coordinator of Graduate Teaching Assistants for the Department of Health Education at Southern Illinois University at Carbondale since 1982.

Joyce V. Fetro, PhD, CHES, is the Health Education Specialist for the San Francisco Unified School District. In that role, she is responsible for inservice training and curriculum development for comprehensive school health education (grades K-12), including mental/emotional health and coping with loss and death. She received her master's and doctoral degrees in health education from Southern Illinois University. Her experience in health education spans twenty years, including thirteen years as a middle school teacher, two years as a university instructor, and three years conducting research and evaluation studies about effectiveness of substance use and pregnancy and HIV/AIDS prevention programs. She is author of *Step by Step to Substance Use Prevention: The Planning Guide for School-Based Programs* (ETR Associates, 1991), and *Personal and Social Skills: Understanding and Integrating Competencies Across Health Content* (ETR Associates, 1992).

Tackle Today's Tough Issues With More Practical Handbooks

(#509-H1)
93 pages/paper/$14.95

(#583-H1)
99 pages/paper/$14.95

(#569-H1)
116 pages/paper/$14.95

(#560-H1)
180 pages/paper/$14.95

(#594-H1)
200 pages/paper/$17.95

Learn a variety of positive, hands-on approaches to help children up to age ten understand the health issues that shape their lives. The Issues Books from ETR Associates. For more information and a complete list of Issues Books...

Call Toll-Free 1 (800) 321-4407

or contact:
Sales Department
ETR Associates
P.O. Box 1830
Santa Cruz, CA 95061-1830
FAX: (408) 438-4284

Prices subject to change without notice.